Sundays on the Phone

✿

Also by Mark Rudman

OTHER WESLEYAN TITLES BY MARK RUDMAN

The Couple (2002)

Provoked in Venice (1999)

The Millennium Hotel (1996)

*Realm of Unknowing: Meditations on Art, Suicide,
and Other Transformations* (1995)

Rider (1994)

POEMS

In the Neighboring Cell

By Contraries

The Nowhere Steps

PROSE

Robert Lowell: An Introduction to the Poetry

Diverse Voices: Essays on Poets and Poetry

TRANSLATIONS

Square of Angels: The Selected Poems of Bohdan Antonych
(with Bohdan Boychuk)

Memories of Love: The Selected Poems of Bohdan Boychuk

My Sister—Life and *The Highest Sickness, poems by Boris Pasternak*
(with Bohdan Boychuk)

Euripides' Daughters of Troy (with Katharine Washburn)

Sundays on the Phone

❧

MARK RUDMAN

Wesleyan University Press
MIDDLETOWN, CONNECTICUT

Published by Wesleyan University Press, Middletown, CT 06459

www.wesleyan.edu/wespress

© 2005 by Mark Rudman

Printed in the United States of America

5 4 3 2 1

LIBRARY OF CONGRESS CATALOGING-IN-PUBLICATION DATA
Rudman, Mark.
Sundays on the phone / Mark Rudman.
    p.   cm. — (Wesleyan poetry)
ISBN-13: 978-0-8195-6785-7 (alk. paper)
ISBN-10: 0-8195-6785-x (alk. paper)
I. Title. II. Series.
PS3568.U329S86 2005
811'.54—dc22   2005010563

For my mother,

Marjorie Louise Levy Leeds Harris Rudman Strome

(1921–1999)

"If you were born a second time you should be very careful, even in your attachment to your mother. You can only lose it."

—*Cesare Pavese*

❧

"Yes, all my life, I think, I had been bent on it. Yes, so far as I was capable of being bent on anything at all a lifetime long, and what a lifetime, I had been bent on settling this matter between my mother and me, but had not succeeded."

—*Samuel Beckett*

❧

"The elaborate fuss that she [Willa Cather] made about cuisine, about wine, and salads, and bread, and copper pots, was an expression of her sense of the unfeeling universe; cookery was a ritual in which the material world, some tiny part of it, could be made to serve human ends, could be made human . . ."

—*Lionel Trilling*

Contents

⁂   III ((Protected) by a Silver Spoon)

⁂   IV

Acknowledgments

Grateful acknowledgment is made to the editors of the magazines in which some of these poems first appeared:

Agni Review: "How Bad Can It Get"
Arion: "Cutting Edge Production"
Chain: "Bonespeak"
The Colorado Review: "Lionel Trains"
Conjunctions: "Birthday Call"
The Forward: "N.O.T.R.O.T.C."
Grand Street: "Cloud in a Bottle"
Maisonneuve: "Starved Rock"
New England Review: "Conversion in Scafa," "Sons and Lovers Recovered!"
The Paris Review: "Back Stairwell," "The Nowhere Water"
Salt: "Sunday's on the Phone," "The Albuquerque Interventions"
Slope: "The 'Emma' Letters," "Late Lunch," "White Woman Singing Scat"
Washington Square: "Patience"

Some of these poems have appeared in the following anthologies or special issues:

First Light, edited by Jason Shinder, Harvest Books: "The Nowhere Water"
The Prairie Schooner Anthology of Contemporary Jewish American Writing, edited by Hilda Raz, Bison Books, University of Nebraska Press: "Approach of the High Holy Days"
Colorado Review, The West, edited by Donald Revell: "Autokinetic Heartbreak"

100 Poets Against the War, edited by Todd Swift, Salt Editions: "N.O.T.R.O.T.C."

"The Nowhere Water" is reprinted from *The Nowhere Steps,* Sheep Meadow Press, 1990.

I would like to thank Tayt Harlin, Aubrie Marrin, and Kendra Sullivan for their invaluable help with the manuscript. Special thanks to Erica Wright. And I would like to add a note of gratitude to Stephen Donadio, Nicholas Poburko, and John Kinsella for their generosity and support.

THE NOWHERE WATER

We ate alone in the immense dining room.
She got me to eat each night
by saying any meat was buffalo meat.
The desert had the silence of one who waits.
Cool water, clear water—*she sang.*
Her voice soothed my deepest blood
as I listened to her sing it over and over;
she knew just how to prolong

cool—clear—water—.
The desert was vast and empty.
Water nowhere, neither cool nor clear.
My one friend lived in a trailer in a dust bowl.
I'd wander off alone and once
got far enough away to where
the bleaching neon of the strip
dwindled to tinsel.

Everywhere we went men were after her.
One clear night we were walking home
hand in hand in the dark.
No moon, but the road was lit
by gas station globes
and not-too-distant hotels,
when a silver-haired man
behind the red wheel of

a white Caddy convertible
stalked alongside
and offered us a ride.
She gripped my hand; panic
coursed through us, our spines rigid.
"Don't look, just keep walking."
Soon she would be married again.
What a waste of beauty—and all on my account.

There is no love like the love
of sons for mothers.
And the seedy silver-haired man,
and his measured, robotic voice,
has hunted me since—
and enters me tonight
through The Talking Heads' searing,
apocalyptic version of the song. . . .

These were the best moments of my life,
alone in Vegas for six weeks
keeping a beautiful woman company
while she obtained her divorce.

I

(KID(S)TUFF)

BACK STAIRWELL

I've chosen to take the stairs.
It's harder, but quicker

than waiting for the elevator
which seems eternally stuck on R—Roof.

And I'm late, the last of the parents
who don't send a stand-in.

I'm running, propelled by a kind of demon
—and embarrassed by my lateness—

up the back stairs of the synagogue,
when a window appears in the shaft,

on the wall of the stairwell;
a real window, like a painting on a wall

through which you can see the sky.
The shattered blue leans in, breaks

through the wall; it leaves
an opening, a sudden shudder, a frisson

like a rustle of eternity
shattered in the vista of receding

clouds, antennae, water towers . . .
and I think we are not far from ecstasy

even in the interior.
I can't get my son to hold the banister

as we descend the stairs;
a look of sheer defiance clouds his face,

the same boy who, the other night
I watched shuffle and backpedal and nearly fall,

down the escalator, over
the rapids of the raw-toothed

edges of the blades;
his hands, his attention, occupied

by a rabbit samurai Ninja turtle
and Krang, the bodiless brain.

I gauged the dive I would need
to catch him if he fell:

a flat out floating horizontal grab
I couldn't even have managed in my youth.

CUTTING EDGE PRODUCTION: MEDEA

(November 2002)

1

Today, at the Columbarium, the rain came down and the wind
bent the slender pine, planted outside the confines, the coffins,

the boughs,

an agitation in the atmosphere so unlike
the muffled drizzle a mere
hundred yards from where
my mother-in-law's ashes were set
down, not scattered, in a hole, oxymoronic, square . . .

2

Medea had no sooner brought her slain
little ones into view than the horripilating electronic screech
at hell level brought the cochlea to hearing's limit;
no one could not have been
dying for the cruel sound to give out . . .

3

It left his crumpled body in its wake.

The young man, his fit having passed—
body slumped in the paramedical wheelchair; head slackly to one side.
He was used to it too by now, the horror,
and the inevitable, stress-induced recurrence—
the seizure, that waited, far from access,
coiled obscurely, indefinitely forestalled but not put off—

an existence composed
of premonitory controls:

imaginary walls; ineffective fortresses; brakes.

4

There is no need for something terrible to happen,
for the worst to occur, as now, for the actors
nothing was really happening on stage,
every night they recited the same lines
and touched the mark.

During the length of a given run the stage actor's life
is repetition: incarnate. Like Los Angeles weather.
Dangerously void of chaos.

Now the audience's many heads craned.
The scene shifted.

The bloodstained smock of the mother,
toga of the father,
torsos of the children.

The cast
froze.

5

In my mental world, someone is always attacking me.

And to confirm the Euripidian
assertion that no one's ever happy
anyway—that this diabolical life
treatise is continually shifting and recasting the terms,

the forms that suffering takes.

An existence constructed around the
                (unanswerable) question of the next

seizure—;

around an agreement that is unsigned

that is tacit from birth:

STARVED ROCK

I want to go back to Starved Rock.
I won't be satisfied until I do.

I won't be the same until I reenact
The battle between the Ottawa and Illinois.

I won't be the same until we've done it again,
Deployed the desolate and unforgiving

Tactic of surrounding the black
Granite boulder and letting the enemy die

Without shedding a drop.
Only biochemical warfare could be as technically sweet.

❧

It was heaven to climb the rock and have
The entire theater of the dead to myself.

I reenacted the battle a hundred times,
Pacing the battlements alone while the paying

Customers played bridge and cribbage in the lodge,
Drew a cruel sustenance from the groans

And dozed in deep cushions,
Captives of the blaze, the Homeric hearth.

❧

I cradled the ball tight to my armpit like a running back.
Tall men and well-appointed women blanched

When I feigned a pass.
And I, who have always been hungry, refused to eat, and fled the
    smoky hall.

Too many words had been spilled over the prime rib.
I didn't refuse to eat because I overempathized with the starved-out
    tribe;

I refused out of disgust at luxury and gluttony and indifference.
My wife's the one with the Indian blood.

❧

This time I won't squander my spirit in a doomed and unvitiate
Attempt to get my stepfather's attention

For a half-an-hour's game of catch with the football
To break the tedium of a long fall Illinois afternoon;

I won't be the only child in a legion of preoccupied adults,
Their minds focused on urgent and important matters

Over which they had no power,
Like the Cold War and the stock market.

❧

I only consented to spend the four-day weekend at the rock
If we could throw the football around.

There wasn't another child of nine in sight,
Even from the high perch of the rock itself.

But there wasn't a moment to be spared from the manic
Intimacies with strangers they must have believed might

Ignite connections, leaven somehow the alien
Air in which they too were strangers. . . .

❧

I want to go back to the black rock of the abandoned
And stare out at the Ottawa tribe as they watch and wait for me to die.

9

I want to go back in time and engineer an escape—go
Through the crevice that led to the underground passageway,

Just wide enough for a girl to slip through to emerge
On the other side and find the energy within to find

Reinforcements to attack the attackers from behind.
Warp the space-time continuum.

And make it mine.
And have the girl who escapes become the bearer of the tale.

And I won't be the same until one of the tribes is called: Black Hawk.
And I won't be the same.

LIONEL TRAINS

What I remember about the Lionel Trains is more how they malfunctioned, how when I tried to unload the cattle from the cars they'd go berserk with electric shock and knock themselves down. And then there was the problem of speed. Who wouldn't want the engine to go faster? If I upped the juice delicately along the straightaway the engine would still topple over on the tight curve. If you're driving a racecar on a speedway, you can push it until you reach the point of maximum tension—and maximum exhilaration as you push against the limits of concrete finite physical possibility. The challenge is at the highest speeds to hold the steering wheel steady. The Lionel Trains were more atmospheric, like the recreation of a western town, but they were not for aesthetic contemplation. It wasn't that I wanted a fantasy car or an equivalent of Phaëthon's chariot to enact my fantasies in a vacuum. Fantasy lacks the gravity to fascinate. It wasn't fantasy, but reality, that I craved. The engine still has to stay on the track, and the Lionel Trains needed more push and give, needed to be able to absorb more stress, in order to remain compelling—something other than a collector's item.

APPROACH OF THE HIGH HOLY DAYS

1

That season's coming around again.

The old questions rear . . .

I'm no longer of two minds.
About this one thing.
You won't see me again
in the guise of a hummingbird
hovering at the entrance
with a borrowed yarmulke
squished in my jacket's side pocket.

Which doesn't mean I've turned my back
on prayer.

I still place prayer in my pantheon.

Prayer is like the Pantheon.

There was a time when I was inside the Ansche Chesed synagogue
every day of the week to fetch my son from Day Care.

What makes you

mention it now? Walking home from our ritual Wednesday night din-
ner at the local Cuban-Chinese I saw Mary Faith, the saint who runs
that institution, The Magical Years, eating alone in the rear of the
Metro Diner (which intersects with Broadway and our cross street).

*You're conflating ancient Italy and modern America: there are no more
saints, only martyrs. Mary Faith is a selfless, hard-working woman who
has devoted her life—*

what we know of it

*at least her later, white-haired years, to the lives of children. But to call
her a saint is inaccurate.*

It's not for her labors; it's my sense that she's spiritually there. That she
answers to a higher order.

(Pause.)

I wonder if she's a church-goer.

Would knowing that bring you closer to the heart of her mystery?

I just wonder if her belief includes formal ritual.

*Go on, wonder, no one can stop you. But please don't say "her belief" as
if it went without saying. Stay secure in your unknowing until the door—
opens of its own accord.*

2

It's my deal.

*I think you think more about prayer
when you're in foreign countries
and you find yourself*

*veritably surrounded
by churches, cathedrals actually
and that makes one hell*

*of a difference, ups the ante
of going in considerably
even if it's to see some work of art,*

*whose content, most likely, is religious,
—Christian religious—
and more sober and solemn*

than any ceremony you're likely to hear
from any living
priest or Rabbi.

You've dealt me a good hand.

You did say one-eyed Jacks were wild?

Why you chisler. . . .

3

(Week of Yom Kippur: The Dentist's Office)

My lips and tongue are slow to get numb.

"What I like about Yom Kippur . . . is that half of it . . .
    takes place . . . inside the temple.
The other half . . . is between
    you and others."

I groan agreement.

"Your pact with your . . . fellow man . . .
   is just as important . . .
atonement means . . .

      are your lips numb?"

Uh uh; tongue.

"I'll take care of that."

Reaches for hypodermic.
"You won't feel this one at all.

To atone you have to contact
the people you've wronged."

I groan disagreement: "What, on the phone?"

"On the phone or when you next . . ."

"What? Show up at the door. Collar someone on the street . . .

You do remember that I grew up in a Rabbi's house? And I never heard anything like this."

"Was he orthodox or reform . . . ?"

4

Appalled.

"You must be numb by now."

Don't interrupt.

You couldn't control me when I was alive and now that I'm alive in another way you have even less power over me.

I submit.

Well you are sitting in that damned dentist's chair 37 stories high over Manhattan and you had to move your tongue while he was drilling—don't interrupt—
> *I bring this up because you feel compelled to talk about atonement with your dentist*

who isn't exactly a Talmudic scholar . . .

no matter how often he flies off to Israel,
spends an hour among the stones
"getting in touch with his ancient past"
and for the rest of the time might just as well be in

Vegas.

Now stand back a minute
from your experience.

Prior to the impalement of your tongue by aforesaid drill,

and the blood he sopped up while making a face that said,
if you weren't such a nervous guy, if you had just kept still,
none of this would have happened

you and he were discussing the coming of Yom Kippur,

which, it's true, I can't think of without thinking of you—

only he had the advantage, when it came to talking,
or m o n o l o g u i n g because your mouth was entering
post-Lydocaine pre-numbness limbo;

and now I must confess that he woke me
from a most powerful slumber—;

and so, forgive me if my bursting in like this from heaven
(I thought you'd like it if I threw that in)

caused your tongue to move at an inauspicious moment.

    After a life spent, squandered, wasted,
among American Jews of the
                            high holy day holiday variety,
the hordes who never set foot in a temple
    except on Rosh Hashonah and Yom Kippur,
I could not let his remark pass unremarked.

Where do these heathens get the nerve to prophesy,

these fools who know no Torah,

who when you say Scholem hear shalom . . .

I can see from your attempt to smile with your lips
stretched to their physical limit and your mouth

like that silent scream in the expressionist painting
you dragged me to see—and I always did what you

told me to do—
that you liked that one.

(Pauses. Clears throat.)

No one should tie practical strings to prayer.

You atone alone, in your heart.

And then, when you're done
        with what is never done,
with what exists only through
        purification,

a continual
        beginning again
with nothing, you can
        reclaim

something of value no one
        can put a price on,
take away, or burn:
        poverty.

And begin—wandering?

It is the nomadic way.

Trackless wilderness.

Wavelike ripples on the sand.

(Pause.)

Why did you never sing this particular song
when you were among the living?

Maybe you weren't listening.

Can I go on, your time in this altitude
is dwindling fast.

Put aside those Freudian notions
everyone treats as sacred scripture now

and forget the small stuff,
the unintentional slights,
the gaffs and faux pas.

It's wishing others ill that does you in.

They come back to me now,
the boiling red faces of your congregants.
The vehemence of their tirades,
denouncing others, never dreaming
the problem could lie within themselves.

Innocent of any complicity.

They lived as if there weren't a price.

I took you along so you could learn something, see how people really are
when they unload . . . on the Rabbi . . . as if asking me also to forgive them
for their petty adulteries, embezzlements and backfiring calculations.

On Passover you raised the ram's horn to your lips, took a deep
breath and let it bleat, rapid, staccato,
like a a jazz player's opening
gambit on the trumpet, to the rhythm of

Ma nish ta nah halilah hazeh shemecal halelos

מַה נִּשְׁתַּנָּה הַלַּיְלָה הַזֶּה מִכָּל הַלֵּילוֹת

I know it cost you to blow the shofar. I tried and couldn't get it to release
a sound other than my own   blowing   and spittle.

So why aren't you in shul?

No other Rabbi's good enough for me.

And I hear that services in London are a bit
like Ascot, a fashion show, the women
wearing enormous designer hats.

"Positively smashing."

*That's not reason enough. Would it please you if they came in rags, or
bent double like that poor homeless woman you're about to espy passing
the shut-down bodega on Broadway.*

I can't justify recoiling from praying in synagogues here.

My friends scattered across America say they go
for the sense of community.
Maybe I would too if I lived in Phoenix or Salt Lake.

I tried to lift you out of the mud. No use.

It is—almost—an element.

AUTOKINETIC HEARTBREAK

1

Afternoon Nap at Camp Wayne

It was just beginning to drizzle when our mail arrived. Can promptness be oppressive, undesirable?

A fat envelope contained a long hand-written letter from Mom—an expert typist—crammed with the usual "uneventful news" before she interjected, masterfully, with no shift of emphasis, that the Rabbi had taken a pulpit in Salt Lake City, we were moving further west again.

I couldn't believe, it couldn't be, it wasn't possible, I had become so happy in Illinois, friends I loved and a quick-eyed, short-haired brunette whom I'd worshipped for three years and had at last managed to dance close with hold and kiss at a candlelit party she held in her basement the night before I carried out my orders to fly east to spend a few legally obligatory weeks "with" my father but "at" his sister's apartment in Manhattan before camp began.

My new life was better than camp. Solitude and company, the world within the horizons accessible by bicycle. Cornfields and black loam, a rhythm of seasons from which I drew comfort and sustenance.

And Chicago less than an hour by train.

I hadn't wanted to leave that final summer but I rationalized, lied to myself, against intuition, already well-schooled in the knowledge that the worst always happens, and forced myself to go along with assumed parental expectations one more year and spare myself the horror of their hysteria and threats.

2

I was also still attached to the kids with whom I'd spent seven summers.

To two or three, though less and less to the super-acquisitive suburban
    Jewish princes
who prattled about possessions acquired and promised Bar Mitzvah
    harvests.

When I received that letter from Luke, whom Mom found an eyesore,
"oh ... the one with the moss green teeth," I breathed relief.

When Karen wrote that she felt the way I had about the night when we
    slow danced
and made out tenderly and interminably at her birthday party in her
    basement
I was flying.

At the real altitude, not a height measured by feet above sea level.

3

Mom had mastered the dark art of dropping bad news lightly, and
threw in the place-name, Utah, altitudinous outpost, the way E.M.
Forster in the *The Longest Journey* disposes of Gerald with one auspi-
cious, dry, uninflected sentence: "Gerald died on Tuesday." Not a word
as to how I might react to yet another move when I was so happily
immersed in life. Her wavelike cursive did not lessen the impact of
phrases like "clean air," "clean-minded," and "healthy environment." I
shook with rage and heartbreak and indignation.

First the lines disappeared, then the letter, and now an infra-red boul-
der pressed against my chest; my ribcage would have cracked had my
rage not risen to push the attacker off and roll onto the floor—lucky
that my slant-eyed comrade Mikey Freedom wasn't there to remind
me that since the space between our cots had been declared molten
lava I was dead.

What did dead matter after another irrevocable sundering?
My body moved through space, appeared to move forward, in step
with time, but this twelve-year-old shell was being devoured,
from the inside out, by dread.

For a life, a landscape I had come to love I would exchange, what?

Night after night the moment when the counselors
switched off the lights   IT   reared up:
same narrow canyon, endlessly winding,
no plants, no water, no people, only
a taut stretch of an abyss above what could only have been

sky,

cloudless, measureless, beyond

language.

SONS AND LOVERS RECOVERED!

Look! We Have Come Through!
— D. H. LAWRENCE

Transmission

Dear M,

I can't express enough regret at this   disaster
can imagine   how you   felt   about to burst and as if to rip
the airbus open   and then when
they wouldn't let you back on to check the seat pocket for yourself
     within
nine minutes and eleven seconds of deboarding
you must have been ready to lose it (forgive unintentional pun)
but take   heart   while my physical   being
my moleskin binding and my graph paper pages have been
trashed   some obscure mythic figure known as Aesacus, the Diver
found a way to transmit

the gist

(we hope the exclamation point is Lawrentian!)

Deep Breath

It was 1960. You were eleven. You and your mother had taken the 10:47
train to Chicago to take in a matinee of *Sons and
Lovers.* That left time for lunch and even
a little shopping [conjecture based on pre-established pattern] at
     Marshall Fields before the 2 pm showing.

You and your mother were happy to be together that day.
Through the first half of the movie (more like a series of stills)
you were (?) [can't break this code, word not in our language] with
     terror at
the father, his drunken, bitter vituperations,
still grimy with coal dust from the mines,

23

and you jumped when he struck the table with his fist
and said "God dammit, woman! Don't cast your eyes on the floor
    when I walk in!"

You endured Dean Stockwell's sanitized performance as Paul Morel
but your attention returned to the flickering darks and lights when the
    camera lit
on Mary Ure as Clara Dawes soon to become his lover

[M: I wish your language had a better word. We have lots of words for
blood lust masked in many ways, even by inexperience.]

and as she turned her head the camera and Morel's
gaze fixed on the nape of her neck and your hair stood on end,

and you were riveted to her diaphanous, evanescent, phantom-like,
    earthy yet mysterious presence,
wreathed in the steam of trains' arrivals and departures

narrow staircases   dimly lit

(in the cinematographic fashion of the time)

as she appeared and disappeared as her passionate
affair with Paul   —   Morel   —   Stockwell   ran   its course

[M: We prefer "When the hounds of spring are on winter traces . . ."]

And now it comes back, after they make it
in the grisly seaside B & B   Clara's face
framed by the brass bars of the bedstead

imprisoned by the un-self knowing inexperienced

                        boy

that led her to say "Is it me you want or just it?"

Nothing indirect about Mary Ure who slapped Elia Kazan's face at a
    party

when he said he'd heard her husband John Osborne "was a fag."

&

(The parts you single out aren't even in the novel I can't read what you
    wrote after that
and I'd send it to a cryptologist except the document has been
    vaporized
from the side pocket of the exit seat where you ruinously stowed
it . . . because . . . a . . . a . . . a . . . a . . . line . . . might come . . . on the long
    flight
though you were in no condition that day . . . still food . . . poisoned . . .
still . . . with cramps.)

You must forgive yourself this loss
my son it's the first notebook you've lost
and it only contained five days of unpremeditated writing
at white heat five hours a day under the straw parasol by the sea
when you were supposed to be on vacation
though I know from your pile of thrillers that you meant
to rest . . . refresh yourself . . . which you accomplished in the water . . .
where you swam out further further and further each day
dove deeper and deeper . . .

If we've decoded your wife's transmissions correctly
you've been good about not losing three things
your keys   your notebooks   and your penis—
and be grateful that the lost day still grows
in your memory and your forgetting . . .

how on the return trip on the train in the dusk
(to the small town which your mother scorned and you adored
because you and your friends ranged out as far as your bikes would
    carry you,
conjure reveries in the black dirt of cornfields,
play catch under the backyard maple,
or dream of Karen and the game of spin the bottle in her basement—

that had yet to occur—

the night before you were kidnapped and taken from your
Midwestern angel forever . . .

never to recover!)

she began to speak quietly about *Sons
and Lovers* instead of as she usually did grill
you on plot details you missed while she became
apoplectic that you daydreamed
"during the most important parts!"
and waved her arms wildly
and made you mad.

On this day she spoke in a calm and low voice about how
while the father is gruff the mother's to blame
she's the one who is smothering the boy's soul
so for once you were intrigued that you had missed
                         the entire
                         point

while possessed with fear of the blunt
                         father

played in retrospect with restraint by Trevor Howard

until your prepubescent hair stood on end in excitation
haunted by the ravishing, harsh and tender   frail yet real

            pale, blonde, Scottish
              born actress
                Mary
                Ure . . .

                         ❧

It was the one time when your mother didn't
expect you, an eleven year old
ruffian, to understand a real
adult film, no one else's mother in a town like that would have taken
    their child to see . . .

I know it saddens you Mark to think how companionable
your mother had been and could be in light of
how she became and even though I am only
antimatter now—not even graph
paper—

   it saddens me too!

You—who wrote on me in such a way that I felt wanted . . .

Yours Truly,

Lost (Moleskin) Graph Paper Notebook

PS

Dear Mark,

*Let me clarify a few points. It was Ure's strength you liked; it was only her
blond hair and pale complexion that made you remember her as ethe-
real. It is not she who is fragile but the actor's craft. It's the same sublimi-
nal mistake Perseus made when he saw me chained to the rock and he
watched the wind lash my hair across my face. But he was just a boy, like
Paul Morel.*

*Do you know that the parts you like best in the film weren't even in Law-
rence's novel?*

Yours truly,

Andromeda

PPS

*We just read Thoreau in "The Change Seminars." And your experience
with your lost notebook makes me think vaguely of something he wrote:
"I long ago lost a hound, a bay horse, and a turtledove, and am still on
their trail."*

Dear A,

I can't find my copy.

Dear M,

Have you really looked?

N . O . T . R . O . T . C .

ROTC struck the wrong chord with me.
I couldn't take it seriously.
I raised the question with my friends, no, they
didn't like it but it was required
to graduate high school in Salt Lake City.
I hadn't thought much about pacifism
by the age of fourteen, but had warred
against war all my life; I tormented
the Rabbi with the question why?
Why why why? A dispute over land.
Was this a reason for a man to die?

ROTC struck the wrong chord with me.
I kept wondering how to be excused.
Asthma would keep me out of the army
but not exempt me from ROTC.
We were required to wear the heavy woolen
uniforms all day every Monday,
but since drill preceded first period
I wore a tee shirt and jeans underneath
and changed in the bathroom—
a simple, elegant solution until a tall
senior crashed through the BOYS bathroom door

while I, now in my tee shirt and jeans,
was stuffing the woolen uniform into my briefcase.
He asked, "what's your name, private?"
"Tom Jones," I fired back.
"That's insubordination," he said,
and grabbed my left arm hard with his right
and marched me down to Colonel Will.
I shook myself free of his grip and glowered.
"Do you know what insubordination means, private?"
They stared, jaws clenched, faces red.
Private—what a joke. "Not telling the truth?"

"To an officer, and that makes it worse.
I regret to say you're out for the year.
Unless you're willing to get here an hour
before school and march around the track
carrying your rifle and infantry pack."
"For how long?" "How long do you think, Private
RUDMAN, until school lets out, is that clear."
When he said "clear" I glanced down at his spit-
shined shoes, saluted, and asked if he cared where I dropped off
my uniform, swiveled and walked away while he,
apoplectic, boomed abuses, threatened repercussions—

ROTC struck the wrong chord with me.
In another life the Colonel'd been a pit bull.
Yet he appeared almost likeable when I glimpsed him
waiting in line at the 7-11 or chopping at a golf ball.
To be fair, I take it back, to be accurate,
I had more freedom to behave this way
than the Mormon kids for whom this was life.
I knew that my real father would take my side
when I said that there was no way I would stay
and finish high school in Salt Lake City.
ROTC struck the wrong chord with me.

CLOUD IN A BOTTLE

"Nature loves to hide."
— HERACLITUS

for Sam, aged fourteen

It's a blankness I aspire to
in the open. Close-cropped
mountain trails, undulant hills
in the gradual falling away.

The silence unreal.
We don't want to move,
not while foxes and coyotes
are out wandering too.

In the dusk the hard, carved
clouds appear
to hold their shape
forever.

My teenage son drops
his cool, opens his arms
and exclaims, wouldn't it be great
if we could just put them in a bottle.

To know that the days grow
shorter in August doesn't
cushion the blow
when the fields

disappear
and we've no choice
but to feel our way
back to the car.

II

(SHE CAME IN)

"Jazz to me is singing what is happening now."

—Anita O'Day

SUNDAYS ON THE PHONE

"Life is nothing but rags and tags, and filthy rags at that.
Why was I ever born?"
— HENNY, in *The Man Who Loved Children*

1

I didn't know how I would miss you.
I didn't know in what way I would miss you.
But now it's Sunday, I'm in southern Vermont,
and I'm staring at the phone.

The phone lies motionless.

I know what you'd say if you were helping me with my homework in
   fourth grade.
"A lizard lies motionless."
We knew a lot of lizards, didn't we, and I don't mean Lounge
Lizards, who would have been more fun
than the professionals who dwelt
in sleek postmodern houses
among picturesque rocks in the high
altitudes of Utah and Colorado.

We both loved the air out west.

And living a mile above sea-level.

You need air to sustain life.

And something more.

2

It's Sunday. The infinite silence of the telephone terrifies me.
It's not even Sunday. It's Saturday, July 3,
and I've lost all sense of time.

It's the nightmare of Independence Day weekend.
The threat of crowds is terrifying too.
The brusque rudeness they bring along with hot

money into the Green Mountain State,
hot money, fast money, new money, internet money,
inorganic money, money earned without manual labor,

by people slinking along in Lauren, Klein and Armani suits
purchased at outlets in Manchester.
When we first came to Vermont, and rented

the cheapest ski chalet we could find
in Londonderry (owned by Diana Douglas and adorned
with photographs of her son Michael, then known

for a part as a cop on TV on a show I'd never watched)
there were no outlets in Manchester;
there were leather crafters and health food stores.

The year after Sidney died we rented a farmhouse on a hill in Wind-
ham—on the backside of Magic Mountain far away from anything.
You said it wouldn't be a problem, except for getting up and down the
steps. You'd sleep downstairs. I warned you there'd be nothing to do.
You said it wouldn't be a problem, you'd bring drawing supplies, char-
coal and paper, and the first afternoon you sat in the coolness of the
shadows on the wooden porch and said, "You know, you guys really
know how to live; I sure don't." After that, the wooden benches and
chairs were too hard. You moved indoors, settled in the kitchen, which
had a view of the meadow and the mountain, went through magazines;
luckily *House and Garden*, *House Beautiful*, and *Architectural Digest*
held lots of interest for you.

When I'd invited you to visit and suggested you stay about four days
you replied more in scorn than in anger: "That's *nothing.*" It was
emblematic of our relationship that you assumed I didn't take into
account that it was a brutal day of traveling for such a short stay. You
took my mention of four days as an insult to you and a sign of disre-
spect to Sidney's memory. It showed how little I cared that you'd been
recently widowed and were now alone in the world. And clearly I had

no idea of what you'd been through during the past five years you'd devoted to taking care of a cancer patient. Because I couldn't solve your problems I was oblivious to your pain. Meanwhile you'd booked an unrefundable round-trip ticket. And would stay two weeks. "Mom, two weeks is too long. Do us both a favor and make it a week." "It's too late, the tickets are unrefundable." "So what?" "I'd have to pay a penalty." "I can't believe you did that without asking." "What do you care? You and Madelaine can do your work. Sam will be in camp. I can entertain myself." And you did, that first afternoon, entertain yourself. After that you assumed a "cute" expression and "peeked in." You'd stand over Madelaine while she was working on a problem and say, "You know, I never really understood mathematics. What is it you're doing exactly." I could hear, even though I had protected myself by locking myself in for the morning behind closed doors. If this sounds cruel, so be it. But now I'm only talking about the hours before lunch, not that we eat lunch. One o'clock approached. "Aren't you guys getting hungry? I am. In fact I know I am, my stomach's growling. I think I'll fix myself something to eat. Would either of you like something to eat?"

3

The Last of the Tea

It's the phones themselves, I'm sure of it now.
I thought there was something wrong with the rotary phone
on my side of the bed when it failed to ring at 10:47 on Sunday
    mornings.

I know there's something wrong with both the forest green
    upstairs phone
and the white downstairs phone in this rented house on Stratton.
How do I know? I knew you'd have to ask.

I'm sick to death of questions. Yet cannot
walk away, when there's a chance to enter.
A clearing. A new order of candor.

I hung around last Sunday afternoon
and it didn't ring. The electricity quailed.
The phone remained locked in reptilian silence.

Tight-up. Laconic as a lobsterman,
and meaner. There's something wrong with the phone.
I almost said it out loud, wait it out.

This morning, after the first night I slept through the night
since we arrived on the mountain a week ago,
I woke, remotely happy, or if not

happy at least relieved that I didn't
wake up more exhausted than when I crawled
into bed around 2 am, didn't

look at the phone, poured a tall glass of Homestyle
Tropicana, poured water in the kettle,
turned on the electric burner that takes

longer than possible to heat up and stays as hot
as the furnaces of Los when you've turned
it off, walked back into the bedroom still

reeling with disbelief at having wakened
refreshed, noticed it was past
11, and stared at the coiled green phone.

It is shaped like a lizard.
It was motionless, silent, inert.
I didn't believe it worked, dialed a number and hung up

when an unfamiliar voice answered.
Then I dialed a number in another area code.
A machine fielded this one and a friend's voice,

ghostly, digitized, echoic, reported
that this was no longer the right number and to call . . .
I slammed the phone down.

The tea kettle screamed like Betty Grable.
My son groaned and rolled onto his stomach.
I grabbed the black plastic handle.

Hot as hell. What was the point?
A Coleman stove would be better.
Fumbled for the paper filters.

Fished the cone out of the sink.
It's the end of the coffee.
And the house was surrounded.

By mountains. Impassive. Green.
I headed toward the highway. The foxes were there:
they waited at the forest's edge under slender

leaf cover as if tracking traffic patterns
before venturing across.
I conjured up a scene I can usually count on

to make myself laugh when things get bad:
it's from *The Great Escape*, Donald Pleasance
is sitting across from James Garner

in the P.O.W. barracks and, without moving his lips,
like a ventriloquist, he utters
this line, "that's the last of the tea,"

and it cuts to the quick of the Englishman's state of mind,
a place where the absence of tea is deeper than rock bottom,
bleaker than nothingness; that without this one small comfort

life's unbearable;
the lower orders don't live without tea;
reptiles, flies, slugs,

they all have access to tea;
no, not the teas that humans drink,
but their own species appropriate tea-equivalent.

4

"Sunday's on the phone to Monday"

Sundays were hell waiting for your call.

And if you didn't call and I didn't call you, you'd give me hell.
Either way, I lost.

You had uncanny timing and called always at the wrong time.
The wrong time being the moment after.

Better than during, yes, but during
I don't answer the phone.

Surely we aren't the only couple who find
Sunday morning propitious for "it"—
what the manuals call "conjugal relations."

And that was true for Sunday mornings long
before the child made finding the right time
a job in itself.

≈

The only other person I can think of who would have called
at 10:47 every Sunday morning is Wallace Stevens.
He had long stopped having intimate

relations with his wife before he wrote "Sunday Morning,"
or not long after.
Everyone I know loves that *tour de force* more than I do.

They slay me with quotations. I hate the ending.
It's so self-consciously "great."
I hate the holy hush of ancient sacrifice.

The woman is idealized, the fantasy of a man
who likes to look at, not touch, women;
who prefers landscapes to people.

She dreams his dream of her dream, he sidles
right up to the sublime like a man to whom it never
occurs that he might not be able to walk

on water, a man who would never
interrogate his own autonomous fantasy,
question its reality any more

than he would question that we live in two
worlds at once—yet they leave me uneasy,
the inner lives he imputes to others,

as if the lawyer in civilian life
was elaborating an eloquent
defense to prove his client's innocence,

while the prosecution remained silent,
like a chess player who knows he's beaten
long before his moves have been carried out,

declining to factor in the human
factor, those sordid truths, those destroyers.
It's lovely though, leaving out the "the"

in the limpid lines where "deer walk upon the mountains"
and the quail's cry is a lascivious whistle.
I'm not correcting mistakes.

I'm in the woods, away from any books other than the few heavy
    tomes I brought,
in my continuous fantasy of losing myself in a long long book for days
    on end,
stopping time; there were many summers when I did lug Stevens's
    Opus Posthumous
with me wherever I went on the planet but now the spine's broken,
and when I open it the pages take flight.

I don't want to be wrong out of arrogance or disrespect,
but this is not about correctness, and the same is true, or false,
about Donald Pleasance not being the actor who recites the line

about the last cup of tea—

let some film scholar or trivia buff put it together that it makes no
    sense
for an English actor to deliver those lines to an American actor,
especially one as un-tea oriented as James Garner.

The Phantom and I liked having movie theaters to ourselves
during matinees in Salt Lake City: space to meditate.

I saw *The Great Escape* every week of its run in a dusty, desolate theater
across the street from pawnbroker row.

Fascinated by Steve McQueen's courage and stoicism,
and how his intimacy with his baseball mitt was somehow key

to his ability to rebound from and entertain himself during
repeated stints in solitary; and how he both kept himself sane

and his anger alive by throwing a baseball against a wall,
probably playing imaginary games in his head.

McQueen's character was said to be a teacher in real life.
Real life: the civilian role we never saw him in in the film

whose high points were doing his own motorcycle stunts,
leaping the fence when there was no other way, like Achilles.

And ok it wasn't Donald Pleasance but James Donald—
ominous, two first names—a mild mannered cipher, another actor

whose face was ubiquitous and whose name no one
remembers—who muttered the tight-lipped lines about the tea.

5

You weren't the only one to begin every conversation
with the conversation stopper "so what's new,"
but you'd respond to the well-intentioned answer
with a dour, uninflected "uh-huh,"

no matter how wonderful or horrible, interesting or dull,
as if the question was only a dutiful adherence to convention,
the etiquette of what mothers are asked to ask their children
in the numberless advice columns you read,

before you recited the entire catalogue of chronic ailments and every
    detail
that made Greenville, Mississippi, or Florence, South Carolina,
such awful places to live:

no place to eat, nothing to see, no one to talk to, no one
who's interested in anything, "all they know from is the beach,
where there's nothing to do. Unless you have a boat.
I call it Myrtle Bitch. So that's the life."

Move?

"Too expensive. Don't know anyone.
Besides, it doesn't matter any more.
There's no life. No point. So someday I'll die
and I won't have to think about it any more."

One morning not long before your wish was realized it had been
a particularly lovely Sunday morning,
just me and Madelaine,
no exotic birds, designer linen, or . . .

when the phone rang, I lay there in that blissful
state it ain't exactly easy to attain,

and didn't answer.

You usually hung up when you reached the Phone Mate
but this time I heard your voice,
you sounded lonely and sad, I reached
for the receiver and said "Hi, sorry, just walked in,"
and you said you had nowhere to walk to even if you could walk
and that in about an hour you'd go downstairs
and "eat some food you wouldn't believe,
you just wouldn't believe it.
It's all fried. All they know how to do is fry."
(Long sigh.)
"It is amazing, fried food for the old.
My students avoid fried food like the plague."
"That's because they're smart.
What did you have for breakfast, Mark? Whitefish?"
"Haven't had breakfast yet."
"Oh. I thought you said you'd just been out."
"I was."
"Oh, I thought you might have been to brunch."
"I hate brunch. It wastes the day."
"It so happens that a lot of people look forward to Sunday brunch."
"Do you?"
"What NOW? There's no one in Florence I'd care to have brunch with."
"What about Sally."
"Oh she's a yenta."
"I thought she was your friend."
"In a way. Not really. I mean we talk on the phone. But I never see her.
I wish I could have some sturgeon."
"I thought I sent you a packet from Murray's."
"Oh that's gone."
"Wasn't it just two weeks ago?"
"So what."
"Nothing. I just thought that a half a pound of nova and sable might
last awhile."
"It did."
"That's a lot of smoked fish for one person to consume in two weeks."
"Well I don't know what you mean by a lot."
"Never mind. I'll send more next time."

6

"Better never to have been born."

—SOPHOCLES, EURIPIDES, WILLIAM BUTLER YEATS,

MALCOLM LOWRY . . . , CHRISTINA STEAD, FREDERICK SEIDEL,

MARJORIE LOUISE LEVY HARRIS LEEDS RUDMAN STROME . . .

Monday's on the Phone to Sunday

Now it's really Sunday. The day began at 3 am
with a tropical rain storm, a hail of spears and arrows.
I woke, and lay awake, ecstatic in the torrential downpour,
watching the distant lightning through the skylights,
and the water pooling on the skylights,
streaking the glass doors and windows.

There's nothing like the threat of danger when you're low.

Why did it have to end?

Who can I complain to now who won't say
"Everyone feels that way"?

"You don't understand," I want to say, "the humid heat
makes me desperate, insensible, depraved,
gives me headaches that won't go away—
and I don't get headaches—
awakens the arthritis that crippled
my aunt and my grandfather and my mother."

Did I complain when it was 120° in Arizona?

Do I not love the alteration of that pulverizing oven
and the bracing shock that comes when you jump in the water
and hear your own skin hiss like meat when it hits a hot frying pan?

It's not just any Sunday, it's the final Wimbledon
final of this century.

The final Independence Day as well.

If you'd been alive to speak to this morning
while predictable Pete was kicking mercurial Andre's ass
you would have asked what special plans we had,
what we were doing to celebrate.
I would have answered, "Try to stay still so as to not keel
over in the sticky heat, and stay away from crowds."

Pretending to disguise your disgust at the banality of this,
you'd adopt a toneless voice to inquire,
out of vestigial politeness, "What about the kid."
We'd work our way through this impasse, this gap
between our perception about how life ought to be lived,
and might have moved on, on to the years
where, as an unencumbered couple, Madelaine and I spent
summers in "the only air-conditioned state"
on Penobscot bay, in Stonington and Brooklin,
and after the parade met for cookouts with friends and the friends
of friends; the summers of solitude and community,

of wading out at dusk in hipboots to gather mussels,
and scrape off the barnacles while we waited
for the garlic onions oregano and white wine
to boil; and you would have said "that sounds like more fun";
and I would repeat that we couldn't find enough for Sam to do
in the particular remoteness and isolation of Maine's
rocky coasts and waters too cold to swim in;
and you'd repeat how you put your feelings aside and sent me
to sleepover camp for two months every year for seven years
from the age of five to twelve so "you'd be around other kids,"

and you didn't understand why we hadn't done the same with Sam,
and I'd repeat how much I loved camp
but remind you that the circumstances were entirely different—
that my father had custody of me in the summers
with the provision that I go to camp.

That it wasn't really your choice to send me to camp.

And you'd pretend not to understand.
And buy time with "oh" and "well" until
you lit on a subject with a less complicated
history.

BONESPEAK

1

I can hear you ask:

"Why are you so sure that James Donald wasn't one of those British
stage actors who took film roles for money?"

"Good question, Mom.

I can't help wondering if the actor is as self-effacing offscreen as he is
   on."

"What do you care?"

"It's how the images on the blank white screen
get mixed up with our own screen images."

"I doubt he cares either. Probably makes a bundle."

"Made."

"My brother made $500 a week during the depression
and that's directing B movies that were shot in a week."

"I know. You've told me"

"I went to Julia Richmond High.
And then—my mother died."

"It must have been awful."

"I went to live with Dad.
You could say he had to take me in.

You know I was unwanted.
My parents had agreed to divorce when my mother Irene
discovered she was pregnant.
I only wish I'd never been born."

"I'm glad you were."

"I'm glad you were too."

"But the Greeks agree with you.
I can't tell you how many
variations there have been
on the line that it's better
never to have been born than . . ."

"You don't have to tell me!"

"I know, I know . . ."

"I know you know. I was trying to say
that you're not alone in your suffering."

"That I didn't know. But I know that when
I went on vacation to Myrtle Beach the people on the beach
were reading Michener, not Greek plays.
I mean when you told me how much you were paid to translate that
    Greek play
I didn't know what to say.
Given all the sex and dirt and gossip in your work
I don't know why you don't write a potboiler and then
none of us will have to worry about

money."

"I would if I could."

"I don't see why you can't. You've got the smut."

"It's part of a fabric; I've a higher
purpose in mind: to transcend the squalor."

"So transcend. And be poor. And never go
anywhere. Some people lead wonderful
lives. The people here travel all the time.
Not me. I just sit alone in my room."

"Do you think that there's a copy somewhere of your mother's
translation of *Phaedra*."

"Not *PHA*dra, *PHE*dra, phe, phe.
No, no, everything's gone."

"But it might be on file."

"You should go to Paris."

"I should go. What, as the Hunchback of Notre Dame?"

"Come on, you're not . . ."

"I'm not blaming you. I can't afford lavish trips.
And I'm in pain all the time. To travel
in a wheelchair I have to have someone
push me around.

(Pause.)

You can't build character in children by
giving them things. The best schools, connections—
nothing matters if you're not right in the head.
My father starved the girl and spoiled the boy.
But my brother wasn't a coward like your father
with his bullshit stories of being in Special Intelligence."

"I saw some kind of document to that effect."

"I'm sure. He probably had it forged."

"Mom! That is so nasty. Not everything he said was a lie."

"But it's true."
"That it's a lie? You can't be sure."

"Neither can you."

"True."

"Then let's not argue. You know he was a fraud."

"But inspired. And he did struggle not to succumb to his demons."

"'Demons!'"

2

Different Face

"I'm not a woman but sometimes I wake
and can hardly move, I'm afraid to pull
off the covers: it's like I had no skin."

"That's nothing, I'm exhausted by the time . . ."

"Can I finish?"

"By all means, finish."

"I'm not sure it's something you'll want to hear."

"So tell it already."

"I wake, and I start thinking of this line
by William Blake: 'Why was I born
with a different face?'"

"What's wrong with your face?"

"He means being different inside."

"I don't see what's so bad about that."

"It's about—feeling more—vulnerable
than I'd like—than is—practical."

"You never were very practical."

"We're not on the same wave-length here."

"How could we be when you're so indifferent
to what's going on in the world."

"If you say so. In the years when we moved
almost every year I thought the less I thought
how deeply apart I felt—how at odds
I was with the values that were set out
before me like inviolable truths
instead of makeshift relative conceptions—
the less I'd want to disappear, escape—
I did my best to be invisible.
To blend in."

"I guess it wasn't good enough
since there was never a time
when you weren't being singled
out for one thing or another,

at first for being smart, because
that's how I made you, see, because
I taught you so much when you were
little, and in those early years

your teachers thought you were different
in a good sense, it was only
later, around the time we left
Illinois that you fell apart,

and you set your mind to getting
away with as much mischief
as was humanly possible
without getting thrown in the clink."

(Pause.)

"I've heard of William Blake.
How much money did he make?"

"Enough to survive."

"But he earned his living from his paintings.
He worked as an engraver, you know."

"I know."

"I studied his engravings. Weird.
I mean compared to Gainsborough."

VANISHING ACT

It's Sunday again and the difficult
end of August: first Sunday
in America since the end of June:

Waking too early from the time
change, it's still twilight in Italy,
we sigh—disbelieving.

It's 11:17 and the phone isn't ringing.
Why isn't Mom calling?
It's an entire

year since the mortician and I
conspired to scatter her ashes
around her husband's headstone

and forgo the urn. He knew her wishes.
And knew she hated the made over faces,
"the phonies, who never paid

attention, when you were alive."
Once she was gone she wanted her remains
to go up in flames, and leave no trace,

like the Etruscans, who built their shelters
out of wood and straw,
and burned them down when it was time to go.

And like the Etruscans she was obsessed
with beautiful objects.
Sunday's just Sunday.

Time out of time.
Earlier this August
I was eating *piccione in cassuruola* in Lucca

and it brought back the Cornish hens
she made for us when I was three,
and a time when she seemed—

quiet, relaxed, low key,
almost—happy.
And thirty, only thirty.

In 1946 Sam Mostel was pursuing a career as a painter. It wasn't just that he was bald, hirsute, and fat; it was the manic unpredictable and embarrassing stunts he pulled, like the time he threw down his hat on 57th St, and danced around it, while passersby gathered, stopped, and stared, until you consented to join him for coffee at Horn and Hardart. I used to think: a major mistake. So what if Zero wasn't handsome, a class act, or a good rider. Many tall beautiful women marry far shorter and vastly less brilliant men for other reasons. Impertinent? How many times did you announce that your two husbands failed you miserably "in addition to being failures and alcoholics"? Or wearily address the air with a toxic mixture of resignation and bitter sarcasm that you could "really pick 'em. If I'd had a brain in my head I would have married that dentist." "The redhead we went to the beach with once?" "Yes. I'm surprised you remember. He wasn't much to look at. Except for the carrot top. I wish I'd listened to my father and taken his offer; then I would have lived a normal life. He didn't try to feel me up on our first date like Sidney did—he dropped me at the door like a gentleman—and asked to see me again. But what's the dif? I wasn't in love with him." "You enjoyed Zero's company." "He was a riot. And a nut. You wouldn't believe. So I married a nut anyway, but not a creative nut, like Mostel, just a wise guy who played with people's minds to make himself seem mysterious, but it was all an act." "Then why did you—." "Because I was in love."

BIRTHDAY CALL

"How are your bones?"

"Ashes."

"Happy birthday."

"Restless."

"What?"

"I'm restless in death.
I want to get back."

"That's a good sign."

"But what's it worth?
What are you doing with your time
other than killing it?"

"Let's see, this week, jury duty."

"That's not what I meant."

"I'm working on . . ."

"That's not what I meant."

"A party. I went to a party."

"What did they serve?
What were the women wearing?"

"Bare midriffs."

(She guffaws.)

"And your wife, was she dressed in black?"

"With a purple blouse."

"Well I wish I could go to a party."

"I thought death was a continual party."

"Some joke. You're very funny.
Did anyone ever tell you that?

That's not the way to talk to your mother.

Right?"

(Bats her eyes flirtatiously.)

"Did you meet anyone interesting?'

(He thinks.)

"The beautiful and animated sister of an actor."

"Well that's very nice.
I'd like to meet someone like that."

"Give her time."

"Very funny."

"Why in LA and New York City is everyone
someone's sister or son or daughter?"

"You know." *(Pause. Scrunches up face. Slurs her words, like a 45 on 33 rpms.)*

"That'saveryinterestingquestion."

(Recovers voice.)

"But you don't have that problem, do you?
You're an orphan, aren't you, Mark?
You certainly behaved like one."

(Pause.)

"I meant the offspring of a famous so and so."

"Was Generatia there?"

"Why do you always ask if she was wherever I've gone?"

"I don't know. She's your friend, isn't she?
I met her at your apartment."

"I only see her on the street."

"Oh. That's too bad.

Maybe you should be more careful to keep your friends."

"You're giving me a lump in my throat."

"Well you do want me to be honest, don't you?"

"We've been so busy."

"That's too bad too.

I think you should write a grand adventure.

Something people want to read."

"A book you'd like to read?"

(—I just have!)

"Now what would you do if you weren't so busy?
If every minute weren't accounted for?

I don't know how you can be so busy.
You only teach two afternoons a week.
Sounds like a swell job to me.

More like a vacation."

(His face grows red. Voice grows hoarse.)

"That's to earn the money to give myself time to write, remember
   Mom?"

"I'm sorry, I forgot. I must be stupid."

(Hits herself on forehead to emphasize "stupidity.")

"I need a day to recover.
It leaves a few days to write and live.
And I need time to waste."

"Well you've always wasted plenty of time.
I never saw you do anything except listen to music in your room.
Never saw you pick up a book."

*(Thump of body as it falls to wood floor. Beats fists weakly on ground.
   Dry tears.)*

"I wasn't aware that you were spying."

"I used to read a lot, and I read to you too, Mark, when you were
   little—
that's how come you know so much—
but now I just don't have the energy.
Or the incentive."

(Pause.)

"If I did write that book I'd write about you."

"Now that's what I'd call stupid.
My life was just one big mistake."

"Thanks."

"I don't mean you."

"Then why are you so critical? So unsatisfied?"

(Assumes little girl/little old lady voice.)

"I don't mean to be, dear."

"Maybe it was the longings that counted.

You were so open in your letters.

What a difference between the honest and anguished
you of your letters and the frowning groaner
you were in person.

Maybe there's an epistolary novel in your correspondence."

"I doubt it. Who would care anyway
about the groanings of an insignificant woman?
No one cares about my misery.

What's so special?

Now your life, that would be interesting."

"Doing what I do?"

"Oh no, oh no.

I mean, you live in New York City and you never go
to any fine restaurants or Broadway plays."

"Not never."

"When was the last time you went to a museum?

You didn't see *Phantom*.
I just don't get you."

(Shakes her head vehemently.)

"I'd go to Broadway plays. Musicals!"

"The Producers?"

"I'll bet that's a howl.

Who the hell can afford the lifestyle?
The stockbrokers have made a killing."

"Had."

"Well, while I was alive.

I told you to study law.
Or medicine.
Then you wouldn't have to run to doctors."

"You did have every disease—except cancer."

"The big C.

(Counts on fingers methodically.)

The psoriasis, the rheumatoid, the varicose veins (remember I had that operation?); the psoriatic arthritis that made the scabs burn; then . . . diabetes, emphysema, and arteriosclerosis."

"The latter three could have been avoided."

"That's probably true, if I had given a damn.

Terrible, terrible stress.

(Lowers voice, mumbles: "And the valgus heel.")

(Let's not forget the hysterectomy that was the beginning of my mood fall; they were hysterectomy crazy in the 60's, those bastards, they just love to cut; I think they're misogynists.)

And of course I swelled up like a balloon when you had the appendicitis."

"So I've heard."

"You don't know what you put me through."

(Visibly upset, she wrings her hands.)

"And the only thing that helped."

(Pause.)

"The swimming.

I was a beautiful swimmer, don't you think so, Mark?
In Beverly Hills they all said I swam like Esther Williams."

(Displays her "effortless, smooth, slow" stroke.)

"I never saw her swim."

"You don't know who Esther Williams was?"

"The swimming actress."

"She happened to have been an Olympic swimmer!"

"No she wasn't."

"Oh yes she was."

"The team was heading for Tokyo when World War II intervened, canceling the games and her hopes for gold."

"Now where did you get that misinformation?"

"The internet.

I looked her up as we spoke."

(She composes herself. Delivers dignified reply.)

"It doesn't take away from the fact that they all said
I swam like Esther Williams."

"Why can't people just be themselves?
Why do they have to look like a prototype?"

"A simulacra."

(Pause.)

"You smile, Mark.

The dead read their Baudrillard."

HOW BAD CAN IT GET

Could the thin air have served as an environmental anti-depressant
    for you?
Were you on a natural high in Salt Lake City?
On your way out the door before I awakened,

bearing your myriad sketch pads, canvases, charcoal pencils, rags,
and brushes galore—for broad backgrounds and eyelashes—
you became, in your forties, a stellar student at Westminster College
    and the "U"

where the artists said "there was no one else" like you.
No one — who could identify — a — Louis Quinze chair — at first
    glance.
Or tell a Matta from a Gorki.

Your immersion in attacking the canvas brought a fresh
gust of wind into the apartment. Along with your portable forest.
With your hands submerged in loam

you hummed to yourself, almost happy.
Happy? I wouldn't go that far.
Being absorbed in work you love is about as good as it gets.

I knew you'd react to that phrase given your reaction
to what happened on the fateful final afternoon of my penultimate
visit to Florence, when I keeled over from a sudden

bug during the matinee of *As Good As It Gets* in the empty theater
in the mall having all but heaved from the sickening smells, rancid
popcorn, disinfectant, or something unidentified but even more
    noxious.

While you devoured the Super Saver popcorn,
stuffing fistful after fistful into your mouth
without pause, and practically hissed

when I whispered that all that salt
wasn't good for your blood pressure,
or your diabetes, and snapped back,

defiant, sarcastic, and annoyed,
"I take medication for that. I can eat ALL the popcorn I want."
Then why do you hurt my ears and tell

me every detail about your chronic physical problems
every time we speak, I wanted to say
as my body slumped across the empty

row of seats where I counted the seconds
before I could return to the solitude of my motel room on the freeway.
You moved with your usual deliberate slowness,

conducting a conversation between you and you
about the virtues of Nicholson's performance.
"Do you think anyone can match it?"

"No, but can I lie down in the back seat?"
You lifted your eyes to heaven and raised your cane.
"That's the life. It's funny, really. I mean really

hilarious if you think about it. You come down
to help me and now I'm taking care of you only
I'm terrified of driving at night.

I'm just beside myself."
"You know the way, Mom,
just drop me off at the motel, I'll be fine."

"You'll be fine! That's a laugh. You, fine, ha!
If you were fine I wouldn't be *famisht*."
"I'm sorry, I'm sweating, I can't sit up,

I thought it was the smell but . . . it's a bug."
"It's a bug all right. A bug. Do me a big favor,
a bug favor, don't come down to 'help me' again.

Help like this I don't need. I think I'll live
longer without your help."
That was a week before you smashed your electric cart

into another Methodist Manor resident—a woman about my own age
with MS who to your consternation never spoke to you again—
rear-ended a truck at a stoplight,

sold the car, bought a new used one—a lemon—
decided you could no longer drive and gave it to the nursing home,
relinquishing your freedom and giving birth to the new

complaint of being stranded, barred from going
out to lunch or shopping or to a movie when the mood struck.
That was a year before you died.

Faint from the flu, I chose to sweat my lightheaded way
back to New York City, fighting for a standby seat in Charlotte
while cared for by several of Delta's blond angels

with soothing, southern voices,
who called me "honey" and touched my forehead
and asked if I was sure I was well enough to fly

with a fever, yet respected my desire to get home as fast as I could.
When you got wind I'd taken Sam to Myrtle Beach not long after
    to play
golf during his spring vacation and not driven inland

to pay you a visit, you unsheathed your spite and penned
a vicious missive about "two skuzzballs, human slime,"
your son and grandson, who had again maligned

a loving, lonely old mother and grandmother,
because neither he nor I were "like the (grown) children
of all the other people in the home who visited their parents

religiously despite inconvenience to themselves. . . ."
I sent this invective back, as I had others, but scratched my rejoinder:
"Mom, you've never shown any interest in your grandson.

You've never—asked him a question.
You should have moved back to New York City when Sidney died
and would you please stop comparing us to those hicks!"

PHOTOGRAPHS NOT TAKEN OF HUBCAPS
IN FLORENCE, SOUTH CAROLINA

I was, of course, fascinated and repelled.
Puzzled and disturbed and preoccupied,
and I ran it by everyone I saw over the next few days
and everyone claimed half-heartedly that they
"vaguely recalled having passed it."
That includes her lawyer, whose impeccably restored
two-hundred-year-old house that doubles as his office is less
than a quarter-mile shy of the disused
railroad overpass, where traces of white and blue paint
had given over to rust yet retained
traces of a ruined grandeur,
and the shacks of the poor were still
clustered together.
The time couldn't have been less propitious
for political and social issues:
I was in Florence to clear out my mom's apartment
in the Methodist Manor where she spent her last two years,
but I was tempted to come back with her
Nikon, take some black and white
photos of the site and interview
the unkempt yet handsome black man who'd sat
motionless underneath the fabulous
display of hubcaps strung along the wall
until a kid appeared with a damaged bicycle;
it was just the kind of thing I would have done with her
and had done with her my first afternoon in Greenville
when she could still walk without a walker—
get around without her motorized cart in the retirement home
where she ran over a younger woman with rapidly advancing
MS who wouldn't look at her
afterwards, not even after she hand wrote her a letter of apology—
and talk about Walker Evans' Depression period
and search my face for a shocked response to the pathetic
off white shanties of the poor blacks and why
women only came out on the porches to escape
the darkness inside.

What shook me was the absence of power.
She invited me to "shoot away, film is cheap."
I enjoyed those outings, mother and son
on an adventure, wish there'd been more good
times, yet that day opened the shutter too wide
and let in too much light as I despaired
I lacked the patience to capture available light
with a machine that made it all appear so easy,
just as while my eye was now arrested by the dazzling array,
the hubcaps, like spare parts for spaceships,
no word came to mind.

SOLE RESPONSIBILITY

Tuscan cooking brings me back to thoughts of my mother. I didn't know that Ristorante La Mora existed prior to a recommendation I received from an American woman who was visiting her Italian aunt earlier that afternoon. I didn't go to Ristorante La Mora in order to bring back the sight of my mother in the narrow kitchen, or the aroma of the Cornish hens roasting in the oven, but the taste of the tangy pigeons made the dinner a double pleasure.

Between the age of two and five Mom fed me steak tartare, calves brains buerre noir, filet of sole, calves' liver and Cornish hens. She must have intuited that because I was little I would like the diminutive fowl. She was right. She hinted that I'd be very happy with what she'd planned to cook for our dinner that night and she got the broad grin of happy anticipation she wanted to see on my face and I had the thrill of having an entire Cornish hen to myself. For her, the years between the time she left Charles and married Sidney were truly between the wars, a respite during which (both then and in retrospect) she appeared to enjoy her life. She liked being a young, single mother. She found a job near my day care and kindergarten.

Having her parents four floors down was a profoundly mixed blessing, with immense repercussions, but it still allowed her a certain degree of freedom. She could always drop me off and they were (only too) willing to have me. (She claimed that her father was under the delusion that I was his son.) She cooked and we routinely ate dishes that are considered delicacies, dishes for which people travel thousands of miles and fork over, scratch that, spend, immense amounts of money in order to eat. Nor did she spend much time cooking after she picked me up. She made the ritual of cooking into a kind of dance in and out of the narrow kitchen, with a running commentary on how these foods were prepared: "You *sear* the brains."

I never understood my mom's enthusiasm for filet of sole and calves' liver—and I never thought before to associate such disparate members of the food chain by shape and mass. Both filet of sole and calves' liver are flat, born to be sautéed. Worse, both are boneless, shapeless, floppy. My mother would speak of filet of sole the way a couturier would go

71

into raptures over the texture of a dark, rich, impenetrable velvet, the way connoisseurs will imbue a bottle of wine of a certain grape, year, and vineyard with magical powers far beyond being able to imbibe the spirit of the place through the fermented grape. No connoisseur myself, I do believe I ingest the spirit of Lucca when I drink the local cabernet, the dark rich wine whose name, Nero di Camiglino, reinforces that suspicion.

Filet of sole, pun inescapable, embedded in the language, was the embodiment of purity. It didn't matter. I didn't understand the hush and fuss that could accompany the preparation of this tasteless fish, a fish I'm sure has a subtle or delicate taste to those who like it. How are they so sure they're getting the real sole and not a pristine filet carved from another flatfish, like flounder or chad? When sole appears on a menu my companion will inevitably be tempted, as if entertaining the possibility that sole had soul, that the spiritual could be ingested through the physical. If they submit to temptation, and accompany the ingestion of these garlic and parsley decorated morsels with small sighs, "how divine," and if I venture a bite, my response would bring me back to the small table next to the kitchen and my mother's sighs and groans of pleasure and my slightly bewildered indifference. This behavior is a charade. Fish and meat and fowl needed bones to engage my imagination: chewing on this tasteless morsel of pulpy fish made me ponder the mystery of otherness. Sole is definable in terms of what it is not.

Now that I look back on it, I can't escape the idea that calves' brains and steak tartar, which most people I've encountered consider either revolting (almost so on principle) or delicacies, became such health targets. Do the "health-conscious" know that the avocados they eat religiously are all fat even if it's "the good kind of fat"? Or that the egg is being rehabilitated, precisely the suspect yolk?

The joke wasn't lost on my mother. It was guaranteed to get her out of her complaining mode if I maneuvered a conversation toward the subject of these "gourmet" dishes she got me to eat uncomplainingly at such a tender age. She would shrug and anticipate the blow with "so who knew?"

ULTIMATE, OR WOULD YOU PLEASE STOP CALLING HIM "THE KID"

Why isn't penultimate followed by ultimate? On our next and last visit I grew desperate. What I hadn't said out loud was true.

And the week before you died I watched you devour a tub of butter after you ran out of bread at Redbone Alley.

"Yeah, I remember when you drove here with the kid to go bowling."
"How should I know it was a restaurant?"
No response.
"Mom."
No response.
And I said, in as level a voice as I could muster over my pounding heart, "Mom, are you still hungry after the bread and steak and salad?"
"No, not really. God knows the kid can't be hungry."
Exaggerates frown, shakes head in disapproval.
"I can't believe he can eat a sixteen ounce steak."
"He hasn't eaten for a long time."

"Oh. That must be the reason. He sure knows how to slop on the ketchup. Tell me Mark, does he eat anything other than steak and noodles."
"Why don't you ask him, he's sitting right across from you."

She lifted her eyes from her plate for the first time since the waiter had set down the basket of bread and the tubs of butter. He didn't need to hear the question again; it was practically the only thing she'd ever asked him.

"Chicken," he said.
"Oh well that's good. I notice you didn't touch your vegetables."
"I don't like vegetables."
"Oh. Well if I had brought you up you'd love vegetables. But I didn't, and you don't."

She was spooning the butter out of the tub while lecturing the kid on proper diet. This was hell and I sure wasn't out of it.

"Your father ate everything I fed him. Oh yeah, he didn't like brussels sprouts. But then I was a gourmet cook."

The interminable hours she spent in the kitchen, getting everything right, preparing "balanced meals," when by the time the dinner hour rolled around her husband was too soused to care, but not too soused to mock her perfectionism from the high chair of his BarcaLounger. And then reward her with a how "delicious it was, Marjorie." I was in my early teens when their interactions settled into a pattern of vicious digging.

I resolved to leave, to identify a finer scene, and enlisted the help of my father to foot the bill for a boarding school. Neither experience nor reading had prepared me for why married people would stay together only to practice subtle and useless cruelties.

All I knew was pain. Like a tree-knot. And that I wanted to go far far away.

And when, the next year, I left, there would be no return.

PATIENCE!

If his mother counseled patience
he'd explode.

If his friend counseled patience
he'd work at it.

His mother commented sourly on his coffee intake,
sighing with anguish and exasperation, flapping her arms wildly,
unhinged, out of control from her lack of control . . .

"always with the coffee. It's no O O g o o d.
But what's the use. I can't get you to listen."
(Sighs.)
"You never listened."

(Shakes head and forms expression of weary sour disgust.)
"If you want to criticize me some
more, go ahead, get it your of your system."
"No."
(Pause.)
"No."
(Voice pitch feigns disinterest.)
"I mean what's the use after all, a word from me, that's what I always
    said, a word . . . !"
"Who did you say it to?"

Who if I cried would hear me among the angelic orders?

"What does it matter Mark?"

Sidney: "Yeah Marjorie, who did you say it to?"

"To no one. That's who."

Sidney: "She's talking to herself."

(Shakes head slowly to imitate dolefulness pity woe.)

Now raising his voice he asks:

"Are you talking to yourself Marjorie?
Are you keeping yourself good company?"

But we band together, he and I, to make the time in each other's presence endurable. She's far away really, on her own plateau of anger. She's possessed by bitterness. Sidney and I know her distemper isn't, can't be, about us. She was always prone to these fits, these funks, these hysterical outbursts.

Her next sentences will contain something about her parents, she'll conduct a dialogue with them half out loud, nodding in assent to her father's sage verdicts that she shouldn't have married Charles or Sidney ("should" have married the carrot-topped dentist) and then she wouldn't have the three of us to do her dirt.

Chorus dances Charleston, chants:

Should should should.

"I married one bottle and then I married another bottle, only I thought I married a Rabbi. I didn't know that Rabbi's came with bottles too but yes they do, do you know that, Mark?"
"What Mom?"
"Oh nothing. I just thought you might be interested in what I was saying that's all, but why should you be, why should you be different, I mean my father didn't give a shit and Charles, well Charles was another story!"
(Pause.)
"Two losers." *(Counts on fingers.)* "I can really pick 'em."
"I'm sorry."
"What's there to be sorry about, I mean . . ."
"I'm sorry that you feel this way . . . that your life is so awful . . ."
"It's not your fault, I mean you're not the cause, don't put yourself out on my behalf, Mark, you never did, could never get you to see reason . . . and Sidney's a shit, just a shit."
Sidney: "Thank you, Marjorie."

"Thank you both for running each other down all the time in front of me.

I feel sick in your presence; this is why
I left when I did and stayed away.

This is why when I visit I want to leave the next day."

Sidney looks at her, aware I'm not looking at her, with a forced smile, which is a fair response to this no-win situation.

Our bodies are too often inadequate instruments to allow us a wide enough repertory of possible gestures to express emotions.

Now, if she had phrased it this way:

"O gentle son, upon the heat and frame of thy distemper sprinkle cool patience!"

Marjy had a terrific record collection, small but fine.

When she told me that George Shearing was blind I would stare achingly at the cover: it filled me with indeterminate longings. I longed for his spare, dusky sound, the empty spaces. Several times when Sidney was out playing cards we took advantage of his absence from the BarcaLounger and domineering presence to sit in the living room, she on her white loveseats, I on a gray paisley chair, and listen to George Shearing together "like civilized people"—as she liked to say—but it wasn't long before I hijacked *Ella in Berlin* and *Anita* Swings *Cole Porter* into my room.

I was always sensitive to the matter of my mother's loneliness, the essential loneliness of her life (to cadge a phrase from Henry James) and listening to music in silence is one of the best ways for people to spend time together, allowing both intimacy and distance. She didn't play these records as background; when she played, she listened; and once in a while we listened together.

These, along with the times I took her to museums, were our best times together because we had something to focus on other than the only two subjects she was ever willing to raise: our life together during my first five years after she left my father and beyond that how miserable the rest of her life had been in almost every way.

Marjy existed in a terrible solitude. She had no one with whom to share her experience. No friends who loved the things she loved, like music and art. Husband One as is well documented was an undiagnosed manic depressive alcoholic narcissistic sun worshiper and with regard to music was only interested in "the three B's" and schmaltzy Broadway hits. Husband Two had no aesthetic sense, was indifferent to music and art; he lived to talk, "kibitz."

And Marjy and Sidney rarely had a conversation that wasn't acrimonious because they had slender grounds on which to communicate. What do Rabbi and Rebetzen do other than diagnose the flaws of congregants?

I don't think I have ever listened to an album more, or learned it better, than *Ella in Berlin* and I could never get enough of her version of "Lorelei" ("I'm treacherous, ya ya, I'd like to bite my initials on a sailor's neck") and "How High the Moon" and when Marjy caught sight of me listening to the song she asked me if I knew the name of what Ella was doing in the part that flushed me with an alpha wave illegal high endorphin rush and I called back over the music "NO" and she called back if I turned it down she would tell me and I did and she said "scat singing" and I adored the name like a key to an earthly heaven,

"da da da da dee dee dee deed um dad um dad um da da da da da deedle de dum de de dum di yoop di yoop di yoop do da da da da da da da da . . . I guess you must be wonderin' what I'm singing . . . a tisket a tasket and upon my yellow basket . . . havin' a heat wave . . . tropical heat wave . . . (repeats earlier scat riff) I guess I better quit while my heart sings . . . how how how how high   is the mo o o o ooooon."

The starry purple cover of the George Shearing album *In the Night* with him seated at the piano—elegant, cool, and blind—wearing sunglasses of course—was so suggestive, romantic yet dangerous. I would have gone to see him play at the drop of a hat. On my mother's album cover, he looked an indefinite age, which would never change, seated with aplomb at his instrument.

Often my sense of time is off by a year or two but for once I can date the origin of my interest in jazz singers and musicians like George Shearing. *Ella in Berlin* appeared in 1961. I was twelve. It's easier to remember the date of a live performance than the "year" an album was released (noted in infinitesimal print on the bottom of the albums).

It pleased Marjy that I was so wild about Ella and Anita. Years later, long after I had become immersed in reading and writing she confessed her surprise (and dismay at what to her signified further separation): "You know, I never saw you read a book. All I remember you doing was listening to records in your room, MY RECORDS . . ."

She also owned one of the few operas I can tolerate, along with those (and all other music) by Alban Berg, Schoenberg's *Moses and Aaron*, probably because it's unfinished, though I think she had it in the cabinet because it was an appropriate addition to a Rabbi's collection, like the latest release by a contemporary Jewish writer. Once I started *Exodus*, I couldn't put it down, and my first exposure to an erotic love-making scene aroused me by surprise. A continual source of guilt or remorse was my failure to do more than riffle another shelf inhabitant, *The Last of the Just*, a title that made me feel like it was a moral failure on my part not to read it, and that it threatened to be boring; and the author's name, André Schwartz Bart, had a no nonsense yet mysterious aura of its own (how to reconcile Schwartz and Bart?). The dust-jacket had a rough hewn yellowish look, and the cover a washed-out green image that made it appear old and wise even when it was new. I regarded the courage implicit in the title *The Last of the Just* as an indictment of my life.

And Marjy, long after I'd left home, continued to range out in her interests; she kept up with rock 'n' roll, the Beatles (*Sgt. Pepper, Abbey Road*), Carole King, James Taylor, all the way to Eurythmics and The Police, albums I looked forward to listening to on my visits south after Sidney was exiled to pulpits in Greenville, Mississippi, and Florence, South Carolina. She did not have time to "sit and listen to music" because she had to "stand on the hard cement floor hour after hour and that's what gave me the varicose veins." It wasn't that Sidney cared much what he ate. His mind was on his pre- and post-dinner cigars and highballs. But a balanced dinner, with everyone seated (and the tv-etc-off-thank-you) was one dimension of family life she fought not to relinquish.

She begged me to take better care of her albums than I took of mine, which often spent the night out of their jackets, hunting for dust and nightmares, or sported scratches from all the times I replayed the same song, something Marjy never would have done, rather than listen to the album all the way through, in her civilized way.

Marjy was right. She was almost never not right.

Judy Garland she listened to alone, sipping scotch and water—in a robe if she remembered to put it on over her nightgown, which became diaphanous when she raided the refrigerator for a midnight snack. On a night I would like to forget I had come home late and she was singing along with Judy, her enormous breasts and nipples on far too copious display, and I tried to make it to my room pretending not to notice when she exclaimed: "boy, can that girl belt out a song!"

Marjy felt obliged to assume the assigned women's role of her time and didn't kick against the pricks. She accused herself of lacking the courage to stand up to her father when the matter of college arose; as late as 1945, he didn't think women should go to college, at least not as if there was a chance he'd have to pay for it. It was acceptable for her to assist in the war effort by volunteering at Father Duffy's canteen where she made several of her few lifelong friends.

My point: she was younger than her years and, as every word written in this book attests, she was born too early (as well as in the wrong family) to have the choice to live a life in which she would have flourished, even if her temperament and sense of unwantedness was the same as it was. There are a lot of functioning, successful people who are not happy in their personal lives but they take satisfaction from their work. My mother "could have been" (for instance), to use a modest example, an art historian, transforming her encyclopedic knowledge into a vocation. She could have spent her days in a wish-come-true factory, surrounded by and immersed in images and objects from another time.

WHITE WOMAN SINGING SCAT

1

An Album By Its Cover, Oh Yeah

It's the cover of my mother's only
Anita O'Day album, *Anita
O'Day Sings Cole Porter*—she's on a swing
grinning like a kid, loose mid-calf
pleated dress, ankles crossed.
And what could be better than to be pushed back
and forth and back and forth
by rhythmic orchestra conductor
Nelson Riddle . . . ;
impish, complicated smile.

If I were Balzac I'd devote an entire
paragraph of adjectives to describe her smile,
her expression actually, while
rocking, with the air flowing freely between her legs—
A skirt is almost a palimpsest of freedom,
more comfortable than suits and ties—
emblems of entrapment—
cages that make explosions difficult.

The beauty of the real is unsurpassable.
The actual title is so much better
than the one I misremember. It's
O'Day Swings *Cole Porter*
with Billy May.

2

Belated

There are no "days" in the usual sense
when you've traveled between time zones
and exchanged Tuscany's dry heat

in which the grape vines and olive groves flourish
for New York City's flattening humidity.
Six hours jet lagged and "in a mist"

as in a song by Bix Biederbecke
which my mother had mentioned not long before the end
I linger in the air-conditioned aisles at HMV

in the hope I might wake after dawn tomorrow,
Sunday.
Nothing catches my eye.

And while my wife is arraigned by a woman
who must bring her up to date on her child's
regressive progress, I wander into the Danger Zone,

close my eyes around the latest jazz
releases, Coltrane with Coleman, Coltrane with Monk, Live
at the Blue Note—but in the Jazz Singers bin

I see your NAME.
You're in a swing and a man is pushing you,
I know every song by heart and all of your

phrasing, Anita O'Day, you whose name
had slipped behind your indelible image on
O'Day Swings *Cole Porter*

singing the blues in a way to take away the blues,
suck the humidity out of the mid-August blues
in New York City.

You cover songs I love and the song
I discovered belatedly, "Ballad of the Sad
Young Men," which might have been,

but wasn't, written by Billy Strayhorn,
"all the sad young men," old before they're thirty,
mourning the end of the jazz age.

The Gene Krupa Story

Spooky to read the liner notes written when the albums
were first released. Especially when I have no idea
who wrote the haunted songs.

And if I weren't a mere mortal, and my physical
expression of surprise and recognition weren't instantly
consigned to my interior, if I were a gravityless
cartoon character, or at least possessed of special effects,
simulation, my eyeballs would have pinwheeled and sprung out
    of their
sockets when, in my reverie in the Anita O'Day
section of the Jazz Singer bin, I read that in her early years (the '40s)
she "punched out vocals"
                              with Gene Krupa's band, Gene
Krupa being—(along with Chet Baker)—the first
jazz musician my generation knew of as children, not
because we listened to Krupa but because of a
tawdry, low-budget yet captivating movie
with Sal Mineo playing the ill-fated drummer.

Mineo worked hard to mimic Krupa's beat,
to "make it look real," but all the publicity
made the film something to joke about.
Not yet ten years old, we were weary of bullshit.

It was an insult to a musician whose hard-earned substance
was equal to his affect; his cool.
The pathos of Krupa's story struck deep.
"Reefer" would make his life hell.

White Woman Singing Scat

Like everyone I know, my turntable is broken;
I can't play the albums that I cut my teeth on,
the albums I listened to when I ought to have been

doing my homework—out of the question
once Ella or Anita incited a reverie,
once I became entranced, enchanted, by scat.

Ella improvising on *Ella in Berlin*,
O'Day Swings *Cole Porter*,
the quick phrasing, upbeat tempo,

until, having found *All the Sad*
Young Men while killing time, I happened on
"Up State": I hadn't a clue as to

how widely she could range and remain
precise, how she could both
stray and be rapid, delay return

with a kind of vocal sleight-of-hand—
ignited by a botched
tonsillectomy at seven—

that left her without a uvula.
Foolhardy risks are as dull as
the straight path.

The trick is to find a way
between—and it's a trick—
in that there's an element of magic.

When my mother said that we should come to her apartment for lunch at noon I knew we'd never make it. I suggested a bit later. "I can't wait that long," she answered.

Now before I arrived at her apartment for a stately and elegant lunch I would have to stop off and get take out McDonald's for Sam who has never been known to eat supercivilized foods. He has just turned thirteen. Everything took a bit longer than we expected and we arrived, somewhat to my chagrin, at her apartment in the Methodist Manor, closer to 1 than 12. The door is open. I looked around: chaos. Utensils, dishes in the sink.

"Oh why don't you just go fuck yourself.

Why don't you just get the fuck out of here and go back to New York City you shit, you little shit."

Oh my god.

"Just go, I don't want to see you."

I'm standing in her living room with my sweet son, a thousand miles from home.

"LEAVE OH PLEASE DO. WHY DID YOU HAVE TO COME?

Well you came, now you can go."

"I'm hungry."

"Well I've put everything away. Including the settings."

"And you put the unused dishes in the sink?"

"Where else should I put them Mark?

"Back in the cupboard? *(Pause.)* They're clean aren't they? You couldn't have waited a little longer and had something to eat yourself?"

"Oh I ate. I couldn't wait."

"That's good." *(Working to extract any sarcasm of tone.)*

"Is the kid hungry?"

(Sam nods yes.)

"I'm sorry we're late, Mom, we had to stop at McDonald's."

"McDonald's! I make A GOURMET LUNCH and he stops at McDonald's."

(Wearing scarcely buttoned housecoat she opens her arms and looks up to the ceiling.)

"Sam doesn't like fancy food . . ."

"He doesn't like the delicious salad I've made! You used to love my salad! You called them 'Mommy salad'!"

"I told you."

"YOU TOLD ME!"

"You won't stop."

"Why should I stop, you're just a piece of a shit, that's all. The whole life is shit so why should I give a goddam fuck."

"Shall we leave?"

"No, no, the kid must eat. He must have his McNuggets, right Sam?"

(Sam nods yes.)

I place the McDonald's bag on the dining table.

Dizzy, reeling, swooning, vertiginous.

When will it stop? What does she want?

"Oh god. You don't mind if I put down a placemat so he doesn't stain the table, it's very fine wood, I think we bought this in," (rubs palms over wood, places forefinger to nose, pushes upward), "Salt Lake City . . . but I know you don't care about fine things.

You don't, but I do. So first we put down the placemat. And then we put a plate on the placemat, right Sam. And now you can have your McDonald's."

(Draws lips around teeth in self-consciously fake smile.)

Sam sits down quietly. I am astonished that he doesn't appear to register the thunderclap. And grateful that he appears to not be taking her hostility in the solar plexus.

"Oh god, look how he splashes on the ketchup! And slurps the coke."

I can feel the tension in him like a tuning fork, holding it in, maintaining control; after all this is his grandmother. But he knows intuitively that this quarrel isn't about him.

"Just a moment, let me get a placemat. Here . . . here . . . here . . ."

I'm dizzy. I know I'm upset, angry, but am flooded with many other emotions; I feel rocked, like I was being hurled from wave to wave and coming up each time after having swallowed too much sea water, choking.

(A TIME OUT)

I can't remember having been this livid.
I look to the ceiling as if God or Moses or Sidney will come to her
    rescue before I end her life—

I'm wincing.

I should down the bottle of Prozac she disdains to take—(on the off chance it might improve her outlook).

Sidney: "She has no control."

"I don't know what I'd do if I couldn't talk to you. This is no fun, no fun. Ah, but we have each other, let's be glad for that."

Sidney holds out his shaking hand. I touch it. A look of indescribable understanding and love passes between stepfather and son.

Okay, there was my mother and father, couldn't communicate with either, and Sidney, who provided an island.

❦

She's back.

"So, no bar mitzvah for you Sam, huh?"

(He smiles.)

"I don't think so."

"Well, it's too bad that your parents didn't *(as if I'm not in the room)* give you some religion."

(Red-faced.)

"Oh mom," I long to say, "why are you such a sourpuss?"

I know people who say their mothers are wonderful and they allow them to manage their lives. Or people who idolize their mothers and flounder in emotional quandaries.

My mother didn't manage my life, but she curtailed the satisfaction I took from my life.

Had all this not been so bitter, I could have grieved.
I could have written a lachrymose elegy.

More in sorrow than in anger.

I could have catechized, and then they could have set it to music,
    chamber music, and
they could have exited feeling sorrowful but elevated—

    all warm inside

instead of gnawed at from the inside out.

She has never asked him a question. Okay, maybe one. She refers to
him in the third person when he's in the room with her.

And after we've returned to Manhattan she calls and says in a confid-
ing tone: "You know, you should send him down here for a week to
be alone with me and I'll straighten him out for you. By the time he
leaves, he'll be loving vegetables and salads with my delicious vinai-
grette instead of McDonald's."

⁂

(2nd TIME OUT)

"Mark, do not forget thy almost blunted purpose, amazement on thy
    mother sits.

You know she has no control.

She's in a frenzied whirl.

Exert your will."

"I've stood here for an hour hunched over the sink, cutting and slicing
and washing and drying lettuce, opening cans, you see how hard that is
to do with my hands."

(She offers arthritic fingers with bandaged thumb—)

"I am still in the bathrobe—

90

Excuse me!"

(Runs to bathroom.)

I don't think she has a moment when she isn't thinking about herself. I've known thousands of people, never anyone like her.

I feel like I'm being eaten alive, from the inside out.

Once we've eaten she decides it's too late to get a movie in before dinner. She suggests we all rest and meet for dinner at 5:30.

Once we're alone Sam and I exchange glances and share shrugs. He reads my thoughts and says:

"I've never seen a person treat another person that way."

We share shrugs.

I imagine what she'd do if I told her that Sam was looking forward to going to the Y to shoot some hoops while she took her afternoon nap.

If she had me to herself what would she do with me? (See "How Bad Can It Get")

THE "EMMA" LETTERS

"You were so open in your letters."
—"Birthday Call"

"Your 'Emma' letter, after you read *Madame Bovary*—"

"Oh I just happened to pick up a paperback.
Have you read it?
It was very good, and you know,
her life and mine weren't that different."

"I know Mom.

I thought you meant *Emma*."

"Well I just call it that. It is about her.

"No, I mean the Austen *Emma*."

"Oh I haven't read that. Is it like 'Emma'?"

"No, but you really get the woman's point of view."

"I thought 'Emma' conveyed that quite nicely."

"It does. Nevermind."

"You know that Flaubert said he was her."

"Yes Mom."

"It said so in the afterword.
I thought that was very interesting.
I don't doubt it.
A lot of men have strong feminine sides,
did you know that, Mark?"

"I think I've heard it."

"Well it's true, I read it in *Time*.

Do you ever read it? Because if not,
I won't renew the subscription, I'll save the $32.50—
I'll get something for myself instead."

"What, SELF?"

"Maybe, maybe. But I have no time to read Mark,
I've been reading the same paperback for months.
No, I have no time."

"What have you got?"

"Shit is what I've got. The life is shit.
It's just nothing, nothing."

⁂

"The cabinet is locked wherein your Emma letter lies."

"It's better off that way."

"No."

"I'm sure you have a locksmith in your neighborhood."

"I'm not sure it's in there but I think so. I know I saved it in a special
file, along with your 'Bottle' letter."

"I don't know why you'd bother."

"They were beautiful."

"Oh I don't know Mark."

"They were."

"Well thank you."

"'Being married to two bottles . . .'"

" . . . unfortunately true. I married one bottle then I married another. Two men who lived for one thing: the bottle. I can really pick 'em."

"So you've said."

(She always repeats everything with the same intonation; it's like listening to serial music.)

(Imagines lonely old woman with widow's hump walking with cane through the aisles of a desolate book store in Florence, South Carolina. The books are on racks. They have a dusty ragged copy or two of many standard classics, mostly Signet. She flips through Madame Bovary, *and decides to buy it, the same way she would any other book, because the subject—female trouble—interests her.)*

"What's the new book on your bed stand?"

"Oh, another paperback?"

"I get that, but what."

"Middlemarch."

"Middlemarch!"

"Yes, it's supposed to be very good, though I haven't gotten very far in it. You see, Mark, no one would have taken George Eliot seriously if she'd been Mary Anne Evans.

I wish I'd been a man. I wish I'd had a penis."

"I'll bet."

"It's very convenient you know.
You see the lines. The women waiting.

It's hell, just hell.
And when you have to go all the time, well . . ."

(Is reminded of the life his mother might have had: at the very least *an art historian lecturing happily at a university.)*

"I want you to know Mark, I'm very gratified that you're not a drinker."

(Ah, what she doesn't see!—though correct in essence.)

"I mean you're not living for the bottle like your fathers.

But you've got to cut down on the coffee.

And you don't stink up the house with cigars. It's disgusting! I made him smoke on the terrace. But your father was the same, always with the cigar. I wonder Mark if they both didn't like to be holding it, if you know what I mean."

"I do Mom."

"All men are like that.
Of course you never smoked because of the asthma."

"True."

"That's good."

(You made such a point that the filtered cigarettes you smoked were less toxic, had less tar than the unfiltered. Watching you suck the nicotine through the filters with a vengeance made me nauseous.)

Now with your husband on an escapist rampage, riding into town after dinner in the teal blue Oldsmobile he steered with a single index finger, "how's that for power steering, Mark!" for a night of cards, bourbon, and cigars in the Rotunda.

"And what distinguishes these distinguished professionals and men of the cloth," you'd confide to me around midnight, "is that they're all a bunch of lushes. I marry a Rabbi in the hope that he might provide what I'd call an atmosphere of quiet dignity for you to grow up in and what do I get if not another one who lives for the bottle. My father warned me about Sidney. We all drank. And I assumed that Sidney was what's called a social drinker, not a lush who lives for the bottle. I can really pick 'em."

I wish I could have—I don't know what. I didn't have a clear picture. Sidney and I were still buddies, on easy terms with each other. And he'd always give both me and Mom a portion of what he won, when he won, which was always. I didn't know the misery he caused her just as she never knew until years later that he'd been fired from the pulpit he claimed to have quit in order to work on commission for The City of Hope.

"But you know who can beat him at gin? Me."
"Really?"
"Oh sure. And he doesn't like it."
"What? Losing to a woman?"
"Well I'm not sure exactly but your father was the same way. They need to have their egos stroked."
"They must know you're smart!"
"Ah but they're big shots. What they are is big shits."

(Laughter.)

"Your father the big shot know-it-all with the aptitude tests, which of course was your Uncle Jack's idea—now he was brilliant. He had ideas, Jack."

(Presses her right forefinger against her temple to emphasize "ideas.")

"I remember him being nice to you."

"A lot of people have been nice to me, Mark. My professors at the University defer to my knowledge. But the men in my life, the men! My father, my two husbands . . ."
"Remember the time Jack and Tillie visited us in Vegas?"
"I do. I'm surprised you do."
"He had about a hundred cameras slung from his shoulders and a bag bulging with lenses and tripods. I could tell by the way he treated you, gently, quietly, and the affectionate way he called you 'Marjy,' that he liked you. Maybe he took the ventriloquist snapshot!"

"I didn't know you looked at it that way."
"I don't know that I do."
"I had a pretty good figure in those days, didn't I?"
"I'll say."
"Mark, Jack wasn't a fake. He didn't have to play mind games or lay on

the charm like Sidney. He wasn't a talker, he was a doer. It was he who introduced the idea of aptitude testing as a business. Your father had an aptitude for selling . . . zippers."

"Oh come on."

"He sold zippers. Then he went into the business. He's only where he is today because of Jack's death."

"He is smart, Mom."

"He thinks he is. I think he's a wise guy really. A smoothie. A good time Charlie. But he didn't have such a good time after I took the tests and came out with a higher I.Q. He didn't like that at all."

(She guffaws. Becomes pensive. Frowns.)

"It's just unfortunate that Sidney's the same way
because he really has a lot to offer."

(Silence.)

"What could have changed a man so much?"

"Maybe it was you who changed."

"I've taken that into account.
His disappointment must have been immeasurable."

"I didn't know you could measure disappointment.
Certainly not yours.
Your disappointment appears to predate experience."

"How would you know, Mark?"

"That early photograph of you with the ball that's higher than you are."

"Ah, the rubber globe!"

"You looked sad about the whole affair.
It's you alone in the void, I mean world, with your transitional objects.
I was for you a failed transitional object.
I moved.

My independence drove you mad as if you loved me only
insofar as you could control my actions.
After that, bitterness and resentment ran riot.

As if I'd been one of the fathers or husbands who'd betrayed your trust?

The rest was blame.

How did you endure it, a life consumed by bitterness?"

"That's easy.

(Pause.)

My plants."

III

((PROTECTED) BY A SILVER SPOON)

THE ALBUQUERQUE INTERVENTIONS

"And mark in every face I meet
Marks of weakness, marks of woe."
— WILLIAM BLAKE

1

"Why Switzerland? What's this sudden interest
in skiing?"

"I've no burning desire to go.
I was charmed by an e-mail."

"You wouldn't consent to the free lessons.
People the world over spend
a fortune for the chance to ski
Utah's slopes."

"Not that I wouldn't go."

"Where?"

"To Switzerland."

"I visited my brother at his private school in Lausanne.
That's where he got his French,
which served him well when they shot
that film about the Dionne Quints
in Montreal—"

"Five of a Kind . . ."

"That sounds right, though who can remember?"

"I'll always remember because I assumed the title
referred to an impossible poker hand."

(Laughter.)

"And the Chan, set in Paris on the eve
of WWII. It was very dark.

Oh who the hell cares, but I tell you Mark
if my father had done a   fraction   for me
what he did for 'the boy,' Bert,
my life would have been substantially different.
If I'd been a boy, he might have spoiled me, literally
to death, as he did my brother.
I never saw Bert smile,
not even when he was riding high
for a few years during the Depression,
when he directed almost all of his films
and was pulling in $500 a week—a relative fortune—
when people were standing in bread lines.
I know it hurt my mother deeply
that he never sent us a penny.
He directed his first film at twenty-five.
Oh Bert was talented, no question, and who
knows, maybe he wouldn't have knocked himself off
if Dad hadn't butted in so much.
I married Sidney, to get you away
from my father's domineering presence."

2

"You do know I was unwanted?"

"Was it that bad?"

"When I was conceived, Dad and Tatiana were together.
He had no interest in girls—in the idea of a daughter.
And he was probably miffed that my mother
used it as a last ditch effort to get him back.
If my mother hadn't died when I was sixteen,

and died so miserably because of her
stubborn adherence to her ill-placed belief

in Christian Science, I might have had
another life. Been less miserable.
Smiled more. Don't I have a nice smile?

(She bares her teeth.)

People tell me I have beautiful teeth.

(Pause.)

But they don't often see them.
I got out of the habit of smiling after my mother died.
I had watched her skin turn green, I know now I should have called
    a doctor
rather than discuss it with her.
I should have called an ambulance the moment I recognized
that it wasn't a cold, that it would not pass.
But that's my life Mark, wrong decisions.
That's why my stomach blew up like I was pregnant
when you had the appendicitis."

3

"Once I went to live with my father, it was all over.
My Dad did nothing but criticize.
He flogged me with newspapers if I came home
after midnight from a date.
And I was terribly shy to boot,
was terribly self-conscious about my breasts,
and my thin hips and legs made them protrude all the more.
And so I walked hunched over.
Men are lucky that they don't have to carry this—weight.
If I'd been a boy, at the very least he would have allowed me
to go to college."

"You should have insisted."

"About college? Oh sure.
That would have taken more courage than I had.
I wasn't the only one, a lot of powerful men
were afraid to stand up to Dad.
No one could argue with him.
He'd done everything, and knew everything."

"That's ridiculous."

"That's easy for you to say.
Because I got you away from him in time."

"You wanted your father's love."

"Oh, I'm sure I did. And there was no one
to dissuade me. Only Bert took my side.
When he saw me pasting labels on perfume bottles
he said, 'this is no kind of work for my Marjy.'
And that's how I escaped that prison.

At least I got a good education at Julia Richmond
High. We probably learned more
than the kids learn in college today.

(Pause.)

Like how to read and write.
Add. Subtract. Multiply.
Oh Julia Richmond was a fine school.
A public school for girls was a giant
step toward equality.
Do you know who graduated
around the same time as I did?"

"Who?"

"Betty Bacall and Judy Holliday."

"And Patricia Highsmith."

"I wasn't aware of that; I thought she was a Texas girl."

4

"Of course I didn't know in advance that   both   your fathers
would turn out to be alcoholics, ok.

I married Sidney because I thought
'who could provide a better atmosphere for a child
than a Rabbi,' it never crossed my mind that this
Rabbi, who I'd only known to drink socially,
was another alcoholic.

I think you were about fifteen when Sidney
began to disappear after dinner.
There was a group in Salt Lake, all local mucky mucks.
And they liked to drink, especially the priest,
and if I commented on his wobbly state when he returned
he'd snap 'what are you talking about, I've been out working.'"

"And what kind of work is that?"

"Interfaith relations."

(Laughter.)

"Who would think—a Rabbi!

(Pause.)

Still I would like to have had a college education.
Though my mother didn't go to college and she translated *Phaedra*.
Into blank verse. For a WPA production."

"I wish I could see a copy."

"At least I went to business school and
attended the Art Students League
several nights a week;
that's where I studied with Mostel.
My father did not like that."

"Why the hell not?"

"Oh didn't you know?
Dad was a great artist."

"Come on Mom."

"Well you saw the painting of the forest he did at nineteen."

"And the dusky river scene with the dock.
Suffused with pearly light on the water."

"I would have said daybreak not dusk.
But you never knew much about early hours.

I don't know which was worse, having to drag
you out of bed or having to prepare two breakfasts."

"I never asked you to."

"Anyway, everything came so easily to him.
He didn't need lessons. He taught himself.
He didn't say I couldn't take classes but he derided
the paintings I brought home."

"It pains me to hear this."

"Think of how it pains me. It pains me so much I could—"

5

"I wouldn't blame you.
My father said he fought with your father
about your art, said he tried to defend . . ."

"He did. But when he couldn't change either
Dad or me, he became very nasty.
Your father liked to mold people. This is not
a healthy approach to life."

"Yeah. He used to say that all the time.
'I thought I could mold her,' meaning you.
I'd say, 'Why do you say it over and over, mold her, mold her . . .'"

"Ha ha. I'll bet he liked that. What did he say?"

"He said he had 'a Pygmalion complex.'"

"Aha! Always with the complexes. Do you think
these complexes attract nut cases like Charles?"

"I never knew how he meant what he was saying."

"And it tore me apart that he spoke to you that way.
He liked to get a reaction. To put people on the defensive."

"He was good at it."

"Oh yeah. And where did it get him."

"He was a complicated man."

"I think your father tried to make himself appear
a lot more complicated than he was."

"An enigma."

"He was no enigma. He conned you into thinking he was one."
"Mom. It's tactless of me to ask—"

"Oh who gives a fuck."

"Why aren't you like this more often?"

"Like what?"

"Like what. Funny. Witty. Perceptive. Shrewd."

"Oh I don't know. A long time ago. I just gave up.
I mean what do I have to live for?"

"What does anyone have to live for?"

"Who should I have conversations with in this backwater?"

"You could have, you could still . . . —move back to New York."

"What? To be broke all the time and unable
to go out on my own for four months a year.
I can't go out in the winter. My lungs."

"When you talk this way
I don't know what to say.
I don't know how to respond,
fairly.

Which doesn't mean
as I think you think it does
that I'm numb to your pain."

"I don't think anything."

"I don't understand why you gave up swimming.
You loved it so much and it kept you . . ."

"I know, I know. I loved nothing more
than being in the warm water,
but it became too much of a production,

getting undressed, and putting on the suit,
and afterwards I didn't have the strength
to get dressed . . ."

"You say you're depressed."

"I know that."

"But it's not all darkness."

"No."

6

"That's the way my father
described his depression.
Joyless, desireless.
World without light."

"But your father was a nut!
Without luck he would have lived
in darkness long before that.

Charles was a charlatan.
He had to drink because he was afraid
that people would see through his charade."

"Maybe being on the edge
is what made him feel alive."

"You make it sound like skiing."

"That's a different kind of edge.
When I looked down, the mountain
sucked in its gut. The way space
curved made me nervous."

"Nervous? You, nervous?"

"The most annoying thing you did
was to make me without a shell."

"Nervous! You think I'm a case?
And maybe I am.
God knows, after all
I've been through. Back to
nervous. Tell me. When
are you not nervous."

"When I'm in my work."

"I asked *you* not the Pollock interview
you read in one of my books."

"Ok, in the trance state it induces . . ."

"Oh I thought you were always in a trance.
You know nothing about finance.
How anyone can attend college and not
take one practical course is beyond me,

absolutely beyond me, but then I

didn't go to college."

7

("Save Me")

(Aimee Mann can be heard in the background singing:

> *"You look like a perfect fit
> For a girl in need of a tourniquet . . .")*

"Mark, what is that NOISE?
Why are you fiddling with the tape deck while I'm talking to you?
Turn that off, it's absolutely horrible."

"I think it's beautiful."

"It's horrible, turn it off, thank you, and stop
whatever you're doing, I just don't know
what is wrong with you, never did, never understood,
something I did, something I didn't do . . ."

(Silence.)

"Do you want me to put on Anita O'Day."

"No. I want your undivided attention and whenever I look
you're somewhere else . . ."

"Can we change the subject Mom?"

> *("From the ranks of the freaks*
> *Who suspect they could never love anyone.")*

"FREAKS!"

(Lights dim, rustling of furniture.)

8

"I know about trances, why do you think
I did all that painting, gardening, and swimming.

I probably loved
gardening more than
I understood, that
was before there were

books about the deep
satisfaction car-
ing for plants can
give people, would you like

to have a garden?"
"Yes. Now. Not before."

"You might find it more
satisfying than
you could predict now.
The kid's almost grown."

"You say the word 'kid' like it was something to be thrown away."

"Well I don't know but the way you dote on him I've never seen . . ."

"Back to you Mom.
I was always in awe of your green thumb.
Your hands deep in the dirt of your potted plants."

"I never knew that dear.
Never knew you cared.
Of course everyone else
who entered the house,
the first thing they noticed
was the green.

Everyone raved about my plants.

Oh I would have loved a real garden plot.

But it killed me to take care of that house,
so we lived in the apartments, and so did the plants,
but you can be sure they got plenty of southern exposure."

9

"So what stopped you?"

"From what, dear?"

"From skiing in Utah."

"Oh Mark I had terrible arthritis.
The osteo and the rheumatoid.
I can't bear to look at my hands."

(Closes her eyes, holds out her knobbed fingers.)

"Even though it was nothing like this then,
I wasn't going to take up skiing at forty,
though I would have loved to. I loved the West.
That space. That air. That vastness.
Not because of measurable square miles.
Because of scale. Mountain heights and desert
depths. Or flatness. I never understood
why you were so wild for the desert."

"The deceptive impassive stillness.
Nocturnal, alert.
The plants conspiratorial.
The nearness of distant sounds."

"You think keeping it watered is easy?"

"What's easy?"

"Easy is snow that melts into basins.
Basins that become the reservoirs of the cool,
clear water we sang about in Vegas."

10

"Wild hotel, *The Oasis.*
Why couldn't we have stayed at *The Sands.*"

"You never change, do you? Always the fantasies.
Well in real life as opposed to reel life we weren't there on a vacation.
You may remember I was getting a divorce,
I put you in Day Care, so I chose something
modest and affordable."

"I was just kidding.
Day Care, the bleak weedy back yards,
a goat tethered to a lone scrub oak, the kids in their own orbits,
spinning."

"*The Oasis* was convenient for a long stay.
It had a kitchenette and it was next
door to *The Flamingo* so you could get your glam
fix by strolling across the parking lot."

"I sure wanted to drive that white T-Bird
convertible with the red leather seats.
Just once, you know, around the parking lot."

"I seem to remember you almost did.
You had that attendant in your pocket.
Making up songs as you strummed the ukulele
you never really learned how to play."

"I knew how to play it."

"Sounds aren't music. You sang over them.
But when you saw a Texan wearing
a white Stetson, string tie, and red snap button shirt,
you'd draw out the last word until something
else caught your fancy, like his white Caddy.
You were car crazy. No, just plain crazy."

(Laughter.)

11

"Of course if you want a fancy car it helps
to have a real job, do you know how much the doctors
around here pull in now, they have separate cars
for all different types of driving,
town cars, jeeps, and two-seaters for when
they can leave the kids at home."

"I know."

"I know you know. But I don't know why you don't
DO ANYTHING ABOUT IT!"

"Destiny."

"YOU'RE TELLING ME!"

"Can you calm down?"

"Oh sure. I mean why get upset now, when it's too late.
You should see how the kids dote on their parents down here.
I know a doctor who just built an addition on his house
so his wife's mother could live with them."

*So this is what she was angling for all along,
a room of her own in our house.*

"You do know how you first became
acquainted with desert sights?"

"Indelibly."

"When you were no more than . . ."

"I know, you don't have to tell me again."

"Then you tell me."

I. *First Glimpse of Albuquerque*

At three or four, I rose from my mother's lap
when the Big Chief chuffed into Albuquerque.

Urchins pushing cactus dolls and pincushions of themselves
crowded the tracks: I reached out, with yearning perhaps

beyond my years, and though my hand found glass—
discovered wandering—I felt drawn toward

the tentative architecture of the Spanish west
and the caressing syllables of the place-names.

Wandering: you have to learn it again every morning;
not to stumble—face flayed, windmilling arms—

like this old Indian in his Victorian
overcoat buttoned to the top in the hundred-degree oven

lurching onto the narrow two-lane highway north
of Cuba, where cars push 80.

Did he once—hawk fetishes? After Cuba,
I change my mind about stopping in Aztec.

II. *The Return to Albuquerque*

I have longed to be in the hills,
these Sandia hills,

and to look down at the sprawling lights
scattered like juniper and piñon,

cradled within the basin with human
habitation ordered and contained

by the plateau; held—cupped—
not rigidly, within ridges;

nurtured, even with this
low yearly rainfall.

What are you waking for
in the hour before dawn,

cracked bones scattered
like the lights of the city.

What are you asking for,
you who demand so much

from this life—wandering
in the desert of invention.

12

"I didn't know it effected you so deeply."

"I told you.

I knew if I could go
further than I could go I would know
what lies on
solitude's other side."

"You may have told me.

(Pause.)

I don't know, I don't know.
But somehow you've erased
all the good times."

"I've told you many times, how the sight of those
impoverished urchins tore me apart."

"What was so special? You'd seen poverty."

"That was later. After you remarried—"

"Then we knew poverty . . .
What the Gentiles call *(raises forefinger)* 'Ecclesiastical Poverty.'"

"That we were in it together and fate
had put me on the train with a future
to contemplate, and put them on the tracks,
beggary blocking out all other thoughts."

"We never told you that money was everything."

"It wasn't about money, it was about
possibility and the lack of it when I first
recognized how determined those children's
lives were before they'd begun to have lives.
Of course I may be wrong in point of fact.
But I identified the same profound absence of hope
in the faces of so many of the kids I came to know—
and in some cases love—in every school I attended.
I'm not saying they were doomed to humdrum
lives after high school, marriages that would
breed children while the couples became
passionless and estranged with nothing
to talk about, other than 'the game,'
what the Bulls or Bears were doing
to the Lions or the Tigers. . . .

Part of what I loved about Luke Douglas—"

("Oh yeah, the little thing with the moss-green teeth
and ghastly freckles."

"That's how you spoke of him always, yes.")

"was the delight he took in small pleasures,
and yes children the age we were then,
ten, eleven, twelve, are like that,

but while basking in the warmth that emanated
from the letters he sent me at camp I'd look
at the privileged princes from Long Island

with their mohair cardigans and tapered slacks
who woke each day with a case of 'the gets' and 'got
everything,' TV's, air conditioners in their rooms,

sports cars the day they received their driver's licenses,
and wonder if it made them happier
than my friends at home whose lives were

improvisations against boredom,
on quiet streets that were there to be disrupted,
where there was more talk about what we wanted to do,

make a team, get a girl, than possessions.
And every day I had to endure a conceited, uncoordinated brat
carry his top of the line Rawlings glove—

which he hadn't troubled to loosen up with a ball in an oiled
pocket under the mattress—pick his nose in right field
then take weak cuts at the ball when at bat.

Many were good at sports the small town kids never got to play,
or learn how to do, like tennis and swimming.
And I thought, I like knowing how to swim.

These pampered darlings did have something
that my friends from the heartland in large part lacked:
an assumption that the larger world would make room

for them unless they totally fucked up."
"We couldn't afford to reward you with material things.
And your father was too cheap."

"But he paid for camp, and I'm grateful,
because I loved those summers away."

IV

"If you want to see what man could do if he wanted to you have only to think of those who have broken out of prison or tried to break out. They have done as much with a single nail as they could have with a battering ram."

—Georg Christoph Lichtenberg

CONVERSION IN SCAFA

"Sickness is not only in body, but in that part used to be call: soul."
— DR. VIGIL in Malcolm Lowry's *Under the Volcano*

Something happened.

I want to tell you.

I want you to know.

I can't talk about it.

I can't talk at all and my voice isn't hoarse.

My voice only becomes hoarse when I talk about it to my wife
who's with me in this St. John of the Cross-esque dark

night of the soul but often

doesn't respond.

So I say it again.

And then I pass out from exhaustion.

I mean total spiritual exhaustion.

The real exhaustion.

I knew who I was and shuddered at who I had become.

I understand the conversions of so many writers I love for the first
time.

And it might not have happened if I hadn't been disabled by air I could
not breathe,

result of freakish late blooming trees and fumes from the concrete
    factory in Scafa,
able to rise from breakfast washed down with lots of espresso
only to drag upstairs and collapse back into bed

hour after hour after hour

in the beautiful emptiness.

From the dawns, which my retina has stored for all time.

To cockcrow.

To the first swallows looping.

And many times I saw you there, in that doorway, saying
embrace the fear.

And have you looked at *Fear and Trembling* lately?

Looked at, I thought.

Fear, trembling.
Shuddering through uncertainty.
Ambition's barroom.
And while walking around with
boundless trepidation I'd think,

Kierkegaard, ok, but the same

thing happened to Jimmy Stewart in *Vertigo*,

he'd known the risks,

and so the worst happened,

but now his life was limited—and not by his language—

and the screenplay limited his fears to heights

but heights also meant a few feet off the ground
as when he stands on Midge's stool to show her

it's ok, it's nothing,

one more step and he is suddenly, overwhelmingly,
overcome.

A cure?

To go through it again?

But how can you go through anything again?

Only when emptied out can you begin again.
And then a glass of wine.

For pure pleasure or to mourn.

For relief from the pent-up blues in the ruins.

My father never had a glass of wine.
Never a casual drink for pleasure with the others.
Only a tumbler at a time.

He mastered the black art of putting everyone
on the defensive with his barbed quips.

Which led to confrontations.
They've come back to vex me again,
erasing any gains I'd made in

dealing with the two sides of his nature right out of the book by Ste-
venson he loved to talk about more than any other except the one by
Conrad.

I love to wear the Jekyll and Hyde tee shirt I bought after I'd taken Sam
to see the musical.

And it looks better now that it's faded and bloody and the colors run
   and blur.

And who is who and what is what.

I regret having sought solutions more convenient
than the one that enabled
the neuralgia-wracked Francis Parkman
to write his history of Montcalm and Wolfe
in a bathtub on a board propped on the sides
(I believe that Wolfe said he would rather have written Gray's *Elegy*
than taken Quebec, but did he really say it in the boat
moments before the bullet entered his heart?).
It didn't solve the pain; it solved the problem.

And I have lost time.

I have wasted time.

Overcoming.

Teddy Roosevelt was my hero, no, my role model, no, my uncle my
brother my father, no, nothing to me at all, but once I was forced to
accept, through the frequency of doctor's visits if nothing more con-
scious, my fragility, Teddy became a figure of Biblical proportions.

It wasn't the ailments, it was that I underestimated the physical diffi-
culties and repercussions.

Why did I care?

I moved around a lot.

I had to find a way.

I wanted to participate.

To make a life for myself
wherever I lived for however
short a time.

Ball.

Let me see: Dad wasn't around, the Rabbi managed two
physical acts a year during the High Holidays,
holding the Torah and blowing the Ram's Horn.

And my passion for mud was unappeasable,
and no amount of asthma, short of asphyxiation,
could deter me from the thrill of rolling in the mud . . . ,
no, not rolling, being completely immersed.

Football.

Looking back, I wish I'd been a textbook introvert and said "only phi-
losophy bucks me up," involved in school beyond the minimum of
what was required and not

                    living for   recess

and what was happening in the street after
school.

It's my fantasy that I could have lived more in my mind's interior, con-
structing sub-worlds to inhabit while my body was elsewhere, like
somebody who really gets lost—and found—in chess or mathematics.

Among the myriad risks some were truly unwise: stupid.

Like saying yes to playing tackle in a scrimmage without shoulder
     pads
with the Utes, carrying the ball into the line just to see what would
     happen.

"Nobody's serious when they're seventeen."

Nobody's bones are formed at fifteen.

An ex-All American guard, Jewish, married to the daughter of a
     family friend, offered:

A Jewish linesman?

I figured he'd watch over me.

Or that they'd go easy on a kid.
Athletes usually did.

Seven years older and seventy more pounds?

Or that there'd be someone.

Instead of no one.

To open up a hole in the defense.

But the guard became absorbed in the game.

—Who knows what game he was replaying in imagination?

They let me pass a few times and I managed a few unintercepted
    incompletes without harm,
so when I took the handoff and stayed right behind my All American
    friend
I hadn't considered that the defensive line, joined
by the linebackers, would converge to upend me at the ankle and as
    I fell
hit me higher and higher, from all sides,
thigh, waist, torso, shoulder, neck,

and when I was down, piled on.

To complete the crush, squeeze the air out.

I didn't mind a new order of pain.

And to lie motionless under the hard-edged autumnal blue.

There were two things I didn't want: a broken neck or to lose the use of
my legs for life.

"Give the kid some time," I heard a voice say out of the huddle, and it wasn't Ned's.
(They weren't worried, good sign.)

Only on the drive home did Ned confess his fear that I might have broken something when I didn't get up and they had to run the next few plays around me. He confessed, quietly, that he hadn't thought they would have played that rough. Later, over drinks, he managed to get a word in over the wild, boozy, and hilarious banter between my stepfather and his father-in-law; he said he couldn't believe that I had hung in there and played despite some brutal hits. They weren't listening, didn't take it in, but I did. And so did Mom, who appeared proud.

But the real danger wasn't in any lack of control
over animal or machine, it was panic, doing the reverse
of what was best in a crisis.

Gunning the engine at cliff's edge when I wanted to turn it off.

Maybe if "Mom" hadn't used so much of her air time warning me what
      not to do
I would have been less reckless, more lucid in exhilaration,
able to pay more careful attention
to where my body was in the physical world.

Sure, Mom had to get the dirt out.

It's like yesterday. When the sky burst open, people asked:
"How can you continue without an umbrella."

I didn't say, "something else I'm going to leave behind?"

If I was going to get wet I wanted to get drenched.

In these dark times my concentration goes and I can't change
gears, switch to something
more practical, consume myself, workaholic style,
in something so consuming it would take my mind off

the repercussions

the question of what would happen.

Economics.

It's daunting to raise a child in Manhattan when you don't have money.

A more modest lifestyle out of the city?

And the boy is adamant about staying.

Maybe it's your fault for playing that song when he was three,

the one with the refrain

"First we take Manhattan, then we take Berlin."

But this July in the rugged Abruzzo something stole my sleep.

In exhaustion, it all comes clear.

The stars so close to the ground.

The way, the way they appear, one by one.

No vasty, vertiginous blur.

The dry, ravaged air that molds
every rock and shrub and crevice and grotto,
every white house chiseled into the Appenine range.

Not that there is no secret to the universe,
but that the secret may not be one
we want to hear.

Mutinous, destitute, monotonous
squeaking in the fields.
Every night, a reenactment.

Some pernicious scent.
It must have come this way to the others.
This emptying. This knowing

that nothing after today will ever
be that way again, calling
for a new metamorphosis.

Hour after hour, duration, blankness, ashen distances,
once in a while a cloud crossing the trees
in the emptiness like a visionary haze.

Silence. Dogbark. The occasional tractor.

That afternoon in Chieti, whiteness.

Immeasurable.

As every night I pray for deluge.

ABOUT THE AUTHOR

Mark Rudman is the author of seven volumes of poetry and three of prose. He is the winner of The National Book Critics Circle Award for *Rider*, the Max Hayward Award for his translation of Boris Pasternak's *My Sister—Life*, and fellowships from the Guggenheim and Ingram Merrill Foundations, the National Endowment on the Arts, and the New York State Council of the Arts. He is the editor of the international literary journal *Pequod*, and teaches poetry part-time at New York University. He lives in New York City with his wife and son.